CW01214490

Longacre Sc.

First printing: June 2011

Copyright © 2011 by Attic Books. All rights reserved. No part of this book may be used or reproduced in any manner whatsoever without written permission of the publisher, except in the case of brief quotations in articles and reviews.

For information write:
New Leaf Publishing Group, P.O. Box 726, Green Forest, AR 72638.
Attic Books is a division of the New Leaf Publishing Group, Inc.

ISBN-13: 978-0-89051-620-1

Library of Congress Number: 2011905688

Printed in the United States of America

Please visit our website for other great titles: www.nlpg.com

Originally published in 1831 by:

American Sunday-School Union

Now known as:

American Missionary Fellowship

www.americanmissionary.org

ENTERED according to the Act of Congress, in the year 1831, by PAUL BECK, Jr. Treasurer, in trust for the American Sunday-school Union, in the Clerk's Office of the District Court of the Eastern District of Pennsylvania.

THE

LIFE OF JOHN NEWTON,

RECTOR OF THE UNITED PARISHES OF ST. MARY WOOL-
NOTH AND ST. MARY WOOLCHURCH-HAW,
LOMBARD STREET, LONDON.

COMPILED FOR THE AMERICAN SUNDAY SCHOOL UNION, AND
REVISED BY THE COMMITTEE OF PUBLICATION.

AMERICAN SUNDAY SCHOOL UNION.

PHILADELPHIA:
NO. 146 CHESNUT STREET.

PUBLISHER'S NOTE

The ASSU, now called American Missionary Fellowship (AMF), has been associated with some of America's most prominent citizens and religious leaders. Included among ASSU officers or influenced by its mission were Bishop William White of Philadelphia's Christ Church; Bushrod Washington (President George Washington's nephew); Francis Scott Key, who wrote "The Star Spangled Banner"; D.L. Moody; Laura Ingalls Wilder; and John Adams (related to both early American presidents), who personally organized over 320 Sunday schools.

ASSU missionaries carried books published by the mission in saddlebags to leave with the fledgling Sunday schools they had started, promoting literacy, education, and the very best in Christian moral values. Though it stopped publishing books in 1968, American Missionary Fellowship continues its missionary work in the United States, extending beyond Sunday school work to include church planting, church camps, and numerous other programs.

http://www.americanmissionary.org/

ADVERTISEMENT.

THE following memoir, compiled for the use of the American Sunday School Union, can pretend to no merit, but that of accuracy. It is taken from Newton's narrative of himself, and his memoirs by Mr. Cecil; and, so far from attempting any originality, the language of the narrative is adopted wherever it was practicable.

The object of this compilation is, to give the principal events of the life of Newton, in a more regular series than they have yet been presented to the public; and to put it in such a form as will render it easy to be obtained, and acceptable to youthful readers. If this be attained, its object will be accomplished.

THE
LIFE OF JOHN NEWTON.

CHAPTER I.

BIOGRAPHY is useful, by giving instruction in more minute particulars than history. In history, a vast group is presented, of which, the separate individuals, however distinguished, are but parts, and therefore make less impression on the mind. But biography presents a single portrait to the attention, and there is nothing to divert from a particular examination of its excellences and defects.

Few lives, perhaps, if accurately related, and especially if we have the means of examining the operations of the mind, and the motives of action, would be without useful lessons: but there are some so full of incident, and so remarkable in their circumstances, that they are highly interesting and instructive.

The subject of this work, was one of those who have experienced great variety of fortune; at one time degraded to the lowest rank of human wretchedness,—at another elevated to a post of high respectability and usefulness: and his history allures to the practice of those virtues which secured the latter, while it warns against the indulgence of those evil propensities which produced the former. From it, also, we may learn, that no character, however degraded, is to be despaired of; though none should rely on it as authority to indulge in sin; since hundreds are destroyed by such courses, where one is rescued. The power of God can reclaim the most hardened offender, but no one has a right to expect it will be exerted in his favour, if he persist in that which he knows to be wrong.

John Newton was born in London, the 24th of July, 1725, of respectable, though not wealthy parents. His father was, for many years, master of a ship in the Mediterranean trade, an occupation which necessarily kept him much away from home. His mother was a pious woman; and as John was her only child, her whole attention was directed to his education. While he was very young, she herself taught him English with so much success, that when he was four years old he could read with propriety in any common book he met with. She also made him commit to memory, many valuable pieces, chapters, and portions of scripture, the catechism, some hymns and poems; which he afterwards found very useful to him, from the effect they had upon his mind. He was, at that time, of a very mild temper, with little inclination for the noisy sports of children; and always best pleased to be in his mother's company, and to learn what she taught him. She had a great desire that he should enter the ministry; and with this view, intended to have sent him to college, in Scotland, when he became old enough. But his mother died before he was seven years old, and he was left to be brought up under very different management.

His father, who was absent at the time of his mother's death, did not come home until the following year. Soon after his return, he married again, and thus John passed into other hands. His step-mother treated him with kindness; but she was occupied with her own children, who also attracted a large share of his father's attention, and John was allowed to follow his own course. Thus left to himself; he ran about the streets with idle and wicked boys, and soon learned their evil ways. Soon after his father's marriage he was sent to a boarding school, where he remained two years, but learned very little, for the master did not treat him well. He made some progress in Latin, but from the hasty manner in which he acquired it, soon forgot nearly all he had learned. When at home, his father, though he loved him, treated him with great sternness; so that John regarded him with more fear than affection; and this sternness of his father, joined with the severity of the school-master, injured his character, and nearly destroyed the good impressions of his mother's care. But his early lessons were not entirely lost; for he afterwards said, that they long restrained him from the practice of vice, and it was a great while before he could shake them off altogether.

The day John was eleven years old, he went on board of his father's ship; and from that time, till the year 1742, he made several voyages; not, however, pursuing this mode of life steadily, but frequently remaining on shore a considerable time, which was chiefly spent in the country. In his fifteenth year, he was placed, for a few months, at Alicant, in Spain, and had the prospect of settling in business there, with a merchant who was a friend of his father; but his bad habits, and restless behaviour prevented this, and thus a favorable opportunity was lost.

During this period his temper and feelings had undergone several changes. While at school he had but little concern about religion, but was sometimes troubled with a sense of the sinfulness of his conduct; and, as he was fond of reading, some impression was made on his mind, by pious books which came in his way. Under this influence, he attempted some reform, and was, for a time, very religious in his own conceit. But he soon became weary of this course, and gradually became worse than before: instead of prayer, he learned to curse and blaspheme, and was exceedingly wicked when out of his father's sight.

All this was before he was twelve years

old. About that time, he had a dangerous fall from a horse, which had nearly killed him, by throwing him within a few inches of a newly cut hedge-row: and, although he escaped without much injury, he was much alarmed by the danger he had been in, and the reflection that he might have been thus suddenly summoned to appear before God. For some time he broke off from his profane practices, and appeared quite altered; but it was not long before he declined again.

At another time he was roused to reflection by the loss of an intimate companion. They had agreed to go together on board of a ship of war, one *Sunday;* but Newton, providentially came too late: the boat, which was to have taken him, was overset, and his companion, with several others, was drowned. He was invited to the funeral of his play-fellow, and was exceedingly affected, to think that by the delay of a few minutes (which had very much displeased and fretted him till he saw the event,) his life had been preserved. However, this, likewise, was soon forgotten; and notwithstanding his conscience sometimes troubled him, he continued to grow worse, until he was, as he states, abandoned to almost every species of wickedness of which a boy could be guilty.

When in his fifteenth year, a great reform took place in his outward conduct, and he became very strict in his observance of the forms of religion. He spent a great part of the day in reading the scriptures, meditation and prayer: he fasted often, and long; and would hardly answer a question, for fear of speaking an idle word. This state continued nearly two years. " But," he says in his narrative, " it was a poor religion ; it left me, in many respects under the power of sin, and, so far as it prevailed, only tended to make me gloomy, stupid, unsociable, and useless."

Such was young Newton's frame of mind, when, in the year 1742, his father, having retired from active life, was thinking how to settle him in the world, and wished him to engage in some business for himself. But John had no inclination to business, and instead of endeavouring to support himself, and become useful to society, he preferred a visionary scheme of life, a mixture of religion, philosophy, and indolence, very inconsistent with any active occupation. At length, a merchant of Liverpool, an intimate friend of his father, proposed to send him, for some years to Jamaica; and promised to take care of his future fortune. To this, John consented; and every arrangement was made for the voyage, but the week before he was to have sailed, his father sent him on some business, near Maidstone, in the county of Kent; and this journey, which was intended to have occupied but two or three days, gave rise to circumstances which occasioned a total change in his feelings and prospects.

A few days before going to Kent, he received an invitation to visit a family residing in that county. They were distant relations, but intimate friends of his mother: she died in their house; but a coolness took place upon his father's second marriage, and John had had no communication with them for several years. As his road lay within half a mile of their house, he obtained his father's permission to visit them; but was so indifferent about it, that he sometimes thought of passing on without stopping. He, however, went; was immediately recognized, and received with great kindness, as the child of a dear deceased friend. His friends had two daughters, the elder of whom, (as he learned some years afterwards,) had been intended, by their mothers, as his wife, without anticipating the events which afterwards occurred to render their union exceedingly improbable. Almost at the first sight of this girl, then under fourteen years of age, he was impressed with an affection for her, which exerted a great influence over his future life. This affection was romantic in the extreme, and though he soon lost all sense of religion, and became deaf to the remonstrances of prudence and conscience, his regard for her, he declares, was always the same; and none of the scenes of misery and wickedness he afterwards experienced ever banished her from his thoughts.

This powerful feeling roused him from the stupid state of mind in which he had indulged, and led him to exertions he would probably not otherwise have made. Not wishing any longer to go to Jamaica for four or five years, and yet afraid to let his father know his change of intention, he remained in Kent three weeks, instead of three days, and did not return to London, until the vessel in which he was to have gone, had sailed, and the opportunity was lost. His father was much displeased with his conduct; but soon became reconciled, and sent him with a friend, on a voyage to Venice. In this voyage he was exposed to the company and bad example of the common sailors, among whom he associated, and his religious habits yielded very much to their evil influence.

During this voyage, he had an extraordinary dream, which is very particularly related in his narrative; and, evidently, with a belief, that it was a direct warning from heaven. There is no doubt that many men of sound judgment believe that God reveals his will to mankind, in the present age, in dreams. That he did so in the early ages of the church is certain; but there should be very strong evidence to induce us to believe the fact of such revelations at the present day. It is, however, impossible to deny, that dreams, like other natural occurrences, may be the means, under God, of producing beneficial results; and where they have such a tendency they ought to be improved. With these remarks we give Newton's dream, as related by himself; though we must add, that it does not appear to have had any beneficial effect on his future conduct, notwithstanding it made a strong impression on his mind at the time.

"The scene presented to my imagination was the harbour of Venice, where we had lately been. I thought it was night, and my watch upon the deck; and that, as I was walking to and fro by myself, a person came to me (I do not remember from whence) and brought me a ring, with an express charge to keep it carefully; assuring me, that while I preserved that ring I should be happy and successful: but, if I lost or parted with it, I must expect nothing but trouble and misery. I accepted the present, and the terms, willingly, not in the least doubting my own care to preserve it, and highly satisfied to have my happiness in my own keeping. I was engaged in these thoughts, when a second person came to me, and, observing the ring on my finger, took occasion to ask me some questions concerning it. I readily told him its virtues; and his answer expressed a surprise at my weakness, in expecting such effects from a ring. I think he reasoned with me some time, upon the impossibility of the thing; and at length urged me, in direct terms, to throw it away. At first I was shocked at the proposal, but his insinuations prevailed. I began to reason and doubt, and at last plucked it off my finger, and dropped it over the ship's side into the water, which it had no sooner touched than I saw, at the same instant, a terrible fire burst out from a range of mountains (a part of the Alps,) which appeared at some distance behind the city of Venice. I saw the hills as distinct as if awake, and that they were all in flames. I perceived, too late, my folly; and my tempter, with an air of insult informed me, that all the mercy God had in reserve for me, was comprised in that ring, which I had wilfully thrown away. I understood that I must now go with him to the burning mountains, and that all the flames I saw were kindled on my account. I trembled, and was in a great agony; so that it was surprising I did not then awake; but my dream continued, and when I thought myself upon the point of a constrained departure, and stood self-condemned, without plea or hope, suddenly, either a third person, or the same who brought the ring at first, (I am not certain which,) came to me, and demanded the cause of my grief. I told him the plain case, confessing that I had ruined myself wilfully, and deserved no pity. He blamed my rashness, and asked if I should be wiser, supposing I had my ring again. I could hardly answer to this, for I thought it was gone beyond recall. I believe, indeed, I had not time to answer, before I saw this unexpected friend go down under the water, just in the spot where I had dropped it, and he soon returned, bringing the ring with him : the moment he came on board, the flames in the mountains were extinguished, and my seducer left me. Then, was ' the prey taken from the hand of the mighty, and the lawful captive delivered.' My fears were at an end, and with joy and gratitude I approached my kind deliverer to receive the ring again; but he refused to return it, and spoke to this effect: 'If you should be intrusted with this ring again, you would very soon bring yourself into the same distress; you are not able to keep it; but I will preserve it for you, and whenever it is needful will produce it in your behalf.' Upon this I awoke, in a state of mind not to be described: I could hardly eat, or sleep, or transact my necessary business for two or three days; but the impression soon wore off, and in a little time I totally forgot it; and I think it hardly occurred to my mind again till several years afterwards."

Nothing very remarkable occurred in the following part of the voyage. He returned home in December 1743, and soon after repeated his visit to Kent; where he protracted his stay in the same imprudent manner as before, so as again to disappoint his father's designs of settling him in Jamaica, and almost to provoke him to disown him. Before any thing like suitable employment offered again, his imprudence in wearing his common sailor-dress, attracted the notice of a press-gang, (men employed in England, to find sailors to serve on board of ships of war; which they do by going about the streets and taking up any person whom they suppose to be a sailor, and carrying him by force on board some ship of war.) Young Newton was taken by such a gang, and carried on board the Harwich man-of-war. It was a time of great danger; the French fleet was hovering on the coast of England, and seamen were much wanted: his father was therefore unable to procure his release: but in consequence of recommendations to the captain, he was promoted to be a midshipman.

He was thus placed in a situation where he might, by good conduct, have acquired respect, and perhaps, risen to eminence; but his mind was unsettled, and his behaviour such as prevented his further promotion. In this situation he met with companions who completed the ruin of his principles, and gradually prepared him for the evil courses in which he afterwards engaged. His chief acquaintance was a person of great natural talents and agreeable manners, but a zealous advocate of the principles of infidelity; who, taking advantage of the unsettled state of Newton's mind on the subject of religion, talked so much to him about objections and arguments against it, that he at length renounced the truth, and embraced the infidel opinions of his new friend. His future life, while he continued under the influence of these sentiments, is a striking commentary upon the folly, as well as the wickedness of those, who pretend to promote human happiness by removing the restraints, while they destroy the hopes contained in the gospel: and those who are inclined to adopt the principles of these pretended friends of liberal education, may here see the practical operation of their destructive system.

CHAPTER II.

The ship in which Newton was thus placed, was ordered to the East Indies; and while she was preparing for the voyage, the captain gave him permission to go on shore for a day, which he very improperly abused by going a great distance, to pay a farewell visit to the young lady to whom he was so much attached. This detained him several days, and although the captain was prevailed upon to excuse his absence, yet he was highly displeased, and never afterwards regarded the young midship man with favour.

At length, he sailed with a large fleet, but a storm coming on, which injured several of the vessels, the whole fleet put back to Plymouth. While there, young Newton heard that his father had arrived at Torbay, which is upon the same part of the coast with Plymouth, to look after some vessels which had been injured by the storm. He was engaged in the African trade, and John thought if he could only get to his father, he might easily be introduced into that service, which would be better than a long uncertain voyage to the East Indies. Accordingly, without reflecting upon the impropriety, or the danger of the attempt, he determined to escape from his ship and go to his father. This he did in the worst possible way; for, one day, when he was sent ashore with the boat, to prevent the men from deserting, he betrayed his trust, and deserted himself.

Without knowing which road to take, and not daring to ask, for fear of being suspected, he walked on all that day and a part of the next. But when he thought he was within a few hours walk of his father, he was met by a small party of soldiers, whom it was impossible to avoid or deceive. They arrested him, and brought him back to Plymouth; through which he was obliged to walk, guarded like a felon; and filled with shame and fear. He was confined two days in the guard-house, then sent on board his ship, where he was kept awhile in irons, and then publicly stripped, and whipped; after which he was degraded from his rank, and all his former companions were forbidden to show him the least favour, or even to speak to him.

As a midshipman, he had been entitled to some command, which flattered his vanity; but now, he was reduced to a level with the lowest, and exposed to the insults of all. This mortification, while it wounded his pride so deeply, took away the little restraint his former station had imposed upon his conduct, and increased the depravity of his character.

Bad as his situation was, his future prospects were still worse. While his disgrace was something new, the officers, with whom he had formerly associated, felt some pity for him, and endeavoured to protect him from ill usage. But they soon began to cool in their feelings towards him, and ceased their efforts to serve him. They were led to this, also, in some measure, by a regard for their own interest; for the captain, though in general a humane man, and kind to the ship's company, was very revengeful, and not easily reconciled to any one with whom he was angry, and took several occasions to show that he was greatly offended with Newton. The voyage too, was expected to be for five years; so that there was no hope of a speedy deliverance from this situation. To this was added the misery of seeing himself forcibly torn away from the young lady whom he regarded with so much affection, under circumstances which rendered it very improbable he should ever see her again.

Every thing conspired to make him miserable. Mortified, enraged, and in despair, every hour exposed him to some new insult or hardship, with no hope of relief, or mitigation, no friend to assist him, or to listen to his complaint. He says of himself, " whether I looked outward or inward I saw nothing but darkness and misery. I cannot express with what regret I cast my last look upon the English shore. I kept my eyes fixed upon it till the ship's distance increasing, it disappeared. When I could see it no longer, I was tempted to throw myself into the sea, which, according to the wicked system I had adopted, would put an end to all my sorrows. But the secret hand of God restrained me."

The ship sailed first to Madeira, and during the whole time, Newton continued much in the same state. Though he deserved the punishment he suffered, his pride led him to think he had been grossly injured; and his desire of revenge was so great, that he actually formed designs upon the captain's life: and this, he says, was one reason which made him willing to prolong his own. So strong was his belief, at this time, in the infidel system he had adopted, that he was firmly persuaded death would put an end to his existence, and that his soul would live no longer than his body. He therefore felt no fear of God, or future punishment, and only thought of the means of making sure his revenge: and the only restraint upon the indulgence of his passions, was the fear of his memory being despised by the individual he so much loved.

He had resolved not to go to India, but there appeared no prospect of any change in his situation, when it occurred suddenly, and unexpectedly, in a way which could not have been anticipated. After they had been some time at Madeira, the business of the fleet was completed, and they were to sail the following day. On that morning, Newton was late in bed, and would have slept longer, but that one of the midshipmen came down, and, between jest and earnest, ordered him to rise; and on his not immediately complying with the order, cut down the hammock in which he lay, and so forced him to dress himself. Not daring to resent this treatment, though very angry, he dressed himself, and went up on deck, where, at the moment, he saw a man who was putting his clothes into a boat alongside, and who told him he was going to leave the ship. Upon inquiry, Newton was informed that two men from a Guinea ship which lay near, had entered on board the Harwich, and that the commodore had ordered two others to be sent back in their place. Newton had long desired to engage in the African trade, and he immediately determined to seize this opportunity of doing so if possible. He begged that the boat might be detained a few minutes, and then ran to the lieutenants, and intreated them to intercede for him with the captain, that he might be dismissed. They pitied him, and made the application to the captain, who readily yielded to their request, and in about half an hour from his being asleep in his hammock, Newton found himself discharged, and safe on board another ship. Thus, by this sudden event, in which a few minutes would have produced a different result, the whole aspect of his affairs was changed, and he was introduced into an entirely new scene of action.

The ship he went on board of, was bound to Sierra Leone, and those parts of Africa, called the Windward coast. The captain, who was acquainted with his father, received him very kindly, promised him every assistance, and would probably have been his friend, had he deserved it. But instead of improving by experience, he seemed to be only hardened, and his conduct was worse than ever. On board the Harwich, the presence of those who had known him in better circumstances, was some restraint upon the indulgence of his evil propensities : but, in going among strangers, he could appear without disguise, and he was even so depraved, as to rejoice in the exchange, because it gave him an opportunity to be as abandoned as he pleased, without control. Not content with acting badly himself, he took every occasion to seduce others to join him, even at great hazard to himself. The natural consequence of this conduct was the loss of favour with his new captain, who was particularly offended by a satirical song, composed by Newton, in which he was held up to the derision of his crew.

When he had been about six months on board this ship, and she was preparing to leave the coast, the captain died, and the mate succeeded to the command. Newton was, if possible, on worse terms with the mate, than with the captain : and he had reason to believe that if he went in the ship to the West Indies, whither the ship was bound, to dispose of her cargo, he would be again placed on board a man-of-war, which he dreaded worse than death. To avoid this, he determined to remain in Africa, and amused himself with many golden dreams, that there he should have an opportunity of improving his fortune.

There were settled on that part of the coast, a few white men, whose business it was to purchase slaves, and other articles of merchandise, in the adjoining country, and sell them to the ships at a profit. One of these, who had come there in indigent circumstances, had acquired considerable wealth, and was a part-owner of the vessel in which Newton then was. His example inspired our adventurer with hopes of like success, and he obtained his discharge, upon condition of entering into this trader's service. This he did, without making any terms with him, trusting altogether to his generosity; a rashness, which he had abundant reason to repent. He received no compensation for his time while on board the ship, but a bill of exchange which was never paid; so that he landed on the coast of Africa, almost as bare as if he had escaped from shipwreck.

CHAPTER III.

From Cape de Verd, the most western point of Africa, to Cape Palmas, a distance of about 800 miles, the coast is intersected by several rivers; the principal of which are the Gambia, the Rio Grande, the Sierra Leone, the Sherbro, and the Messurado. The Rio Grande, like the Nile, divides into many branches near the sea. On the most northerly, called Cacheo, the Portuguese had a settlement. The southern, called Rio Nuna was, at that time, the usual northern boundary of the white men's trade. Sierra Leone is a mountainous peninsula; then uninhabited, and thought inaccessible, on account of the thickness of the forests: but it has since been made the site of the English settlement, founded for the purpose of promoting the abolition of slavery. About twelve leagues to the south east of this, are three contiguous islands, called the Bananoes, which were the centre of the white men's residence. Seven leagues further on, lie the Plantanes, three small islands, two miles distant from the continent, at the point which forms one side of the river Sherbro. It was here, that Newton spent the two following years; the greater part of the time, in a state as wretched as can well be conceived; exposed to want of every kind, and reduced to the condition of a slave.

His master had formerly resided at Cape Mount; but had just removed to the Plantanes, and settled upon the largest of the three islands, where they immediately began to build a house, and enter upon trade. Newton now felt some desire to retrieve his lost time, and apply with diligence to his new occupation. In this he might have succeeded pretty well, but for some untoward circumstances, which frustrated his plans, and reduced him to the greatest misery.

His master was very much under the influence of a native woman, who lived with him as a wife. This woman was, from the first, strongly prejudiced against Newton, and used her influence to injure him with his master. It so happened, that he was taken very sick, soon after he landed, and before he had an opportunity of rendering himself useful;

which increased the prejudice against him. While he was sick, his master sailed up the coast, on a trading expedition, and left him in the charge of this woman.

At first, she took some care of him; but as he did not recover very soon, she grew weary, and entirely neglected him. He had, sometimes, great difficulty to procure a drink of cold water, when burning with fever. His bed was a mat, spread upon a board; and a log of wood was his pillow. When his fever left him, and his appetite returned, it was with great difficulty he could get any thing to eat. His negro mistress lived in great plenty herself, but scarcely allowed him sufficient to sustain life; except occasionally, when, in a very good humour, she would send him victuals in her own plate, after she had dined; which he received with the same eagerness that a needy beggar would alms.

Once, when he was called to receive his allowance, he was so weak, that he let the plate fall, and lost the food, to his great disappointment, as she only laughed at his misfortune; and, though the table was covered with dishes, would not permit him to have any more. His distress at times was so great, as to compel him to go by night, and pull up roots in the plantation, (at the risk of being punished as a thief,) and eat them raw, upon the spot, for fear of discovery. These roots were very good, when boiled or roasted, but very unfit to be eaten raw; and the consequence was, that they almost invariably disagreed with his stomach, so that he could not retain them; yet necessity urged him to repeat the experiment. Sometimes he was relieved by strangers, and sometimes, even by the slaves, the victims of cruel avarice, who were touched with pity, and secretly brought him food from their own slender pittance.

To increase his misery, he was exposed to scorn, and contempt. When he was recovering, his mistress would occasionally visit him, to insult him, and enjoy his weakness. She would then call him indolent, and worthless, and compel him to walk; which, when he could hardly do, she would set her attendants to mimic his motions; laugh, clap their hands, and throw limes or even stones at him. But in general, though all who depended on her favour, must join in her treatment, yet when she was out of sight, he was rather pitied, than insulted, by the meanest of her slaves.

At length, his master returned from his voyage, and he complained of this ill usage; but he was not believed, and as he did it in the woman's presence, his condition was not improved for it. When his master went on a second voyage, he took Newton with him, and they did pretty well for a while, till a brother trader they met with, persuaded his master that he was unfaithful, and stole his goods in the night, or while he was on shore. This was almost the only vice with which he could not be justly charged; for he still continued honest, and had always been true, as far as he had been trusted, though he had been exposed to great temptation. But the charge was believed, and he was condemned without evidence.

From that time, his master, also, used him with great harshness. Whenever he left the vessel, Newton was chained upon deck, with a pint of rice, for his day's allowance; which was not increased when his master's absence was prolonged. Sometimes he would have been nearly starved, but for the fish he chanced to catch. When birds were killed, he was seldom allowed any part but the entrails, to bait his hooks with; and at slack water when the current was still, (the only time when it was practicable,) he generally used to fish. If he succeeded, he was greatly rejoiced; and the fish, hastily boiled, or rather, half burned, without salt, or bread, afforded him a delicious meal. If he caught none, he might, if he could, sleep away his hunger, till the next return of slack water, and then try again.

Nor did he suffer less from the inclemency of the weather, and the want of clothes. The rainy season, which is the winter of that climate, was approaching, and his whole suit consisted of a shirt, a pair of trowsers, a cotton handkerchief instead of a cap, and a cotton cloth, about two yards long, to supply the place of upper garments. Thus accoutred, he was exposed for twenty, thirty, and sometimes, even forty hours together, to incessant rains, accompanied with violent gales of wind, without the least shelter, while his master was on shore. This exposure broke down his spirit, and injured his constitution, to such a degree that he never entirely recovered from the effects of it.

In about two months, they returned from this expedition, and the rest of the time he remained with this man, was chiefly spent at the Plantanes; where he continued much in the same situation as before, subject to the whims and caprices of his cruel mistress. He was now completely subdued. But he was not improved by adversity. He no longer felt the violent passions of rage, or despair, which filled him while on board the Harwich; but he had lost all resolution, and almost all reflection; and his recovery appeared nearly hopeless.

Yet, even in this miserable condition; desstitute of food, and clothing, and reduced to the lowest stage of human wretchedness, he retained some recollection of his mathematical studies, and could, sometimes, sufficiently collect his mind to attend to them. He had with him, a copy of Barrow's Euclid, which he had brought from England. This was his only solace; and while drawing diagrams in the sand, in some remote corner of the island, he could, for a while, beguile his sorrows, and almost forget that he was a forlorn, degraded outcast.

His situation at this period, and the feelings with which he afterwards reverted to it, are best described in his own words.

" I remember that in some of those mournful days, to which my last letter refers, I was busied in planting some lime or lemon trees. The plants I put into the ground were no larger than a young gooseberry bush; my master and his mistress passing by the place, stopped a while to look at me; at last, " who knows," says he, " who knows but by the time these trees grow up and bear, you may go home to England, obtain the command of a ship, and return to reap the fruits of your labours; we see strange things sometimes happen." This, as he intended it, was a cutting sarcasm. I believe he thought it full as probable, that I should live to be king of Poland; yet it proved a prediction, and they (one of them at least,) lived to see me return from England in the capacity he had mentioned, and pluck some of the first limes from those very trees. How can I proceed in my relation, till I raise a monument to the divine goodness, by comparing the circumstances in which the Lord has since placed me, with what I was at that time! Had you seen me, Sir, then, go so pensive and solitary, in the dead of night, to wash my one shirt upon the rocks, and afterwards put it on wet, that it might dry upon my back, while I slept; had you seen me so poor a figure, that when a ship's boat came to the island, shame often constrained me to hide myself in the woods, from the sight of strangers; especially, had you known that my conduct, principles, and heart, were still darker than my outward condition, how little would you have imagined, that one, who so fully answered to the στυγητοι και μισουντες,* of the apostle, was reserved to be so peculiar an instance of the providential care and exuberant goodness of God. There was, at that time, but one earnest desire in my heart, which was not contrary and shocking both to religion and reason; that one desire, though my vile licentious life rendered me peculiarly unworthy of success, and though

* Hateful and hating one another.

a thousand difficulties seemed to render it impossible, the Lord was pleased to gratify. But this favour, though great, and greatly prized, was a small thing compared to the blessings of his grace; he spared me, to give me the knowledge of himself, in the person of Jesus Christ; in love to my soul he delivered me from the pit of corruption, and cast all my aggravated sins behind his back. He brought my feet into the paths of peace. This is indeed the chief article, but it is not the whole. When he made me acceptable to himself in the beloved, he gave me favour in the sight of others. He raised me new friends, protected and guided me through a long series of dangers, and crowned every day with repeated mercies. To him I owe it, that I am still alive, and that I am not still living in hunger, and in thirst, and in nakedness, and the want of all things : into that state I brought myself, but it was he who delivered me. He has given me an easy situation in life, some experimental knowledge of his gospel, a large acquaintance amongst his people, a friendship and correspondence with several of his most honoured servants. But it is as difficult to enumerate my present advantages, as it is fully to describe the evils and miseries of the preceding contrast."

The whole time he remained with this master, was about one year. During this period, he wrote several times to his father, describing his condition, and requesting assistance; at the same time, intimating that he would not return to England, unless his father sent for him. When informed of his situation, his father applied to a friend in Liverpool, who was then fitting out a ship for the coast of Africa; and who, accordingly, gave orders to his captain, to find out Newton, and bring him back to England.

In the meantime, Newton had obtained his master's consent to leave him, and enter the service of another trader, who lived on the same island. This change was greatly to his advantage. He was soon decently clothed, lived in plenty, was treated as a companion, and entrusted with the care of all his new master's domestic effects, to the amount of some thousand pounds.

This man had several factories or agencies in different places. To one of these, situated at Kittam, near the sea, Newton was sent, after a short time; and there, he had a share in the management of business, jointly with another of his master's servants. They lived as they pleased, business flourished, and their employer was satisfied.

Of this period he says, " here I began to be wretch enough to think myself happy. There is a significant phrase frequently used in those parts, " that such a white man is grown black." It does not intend an alteration of complexion, but disposition. I have known several, who, settling in Africa after the age of thirty or forty, have, at that time of life, been gradually assimilated to the tempers, customs, and ceremonies of the natives, so far as to prefer that country to England; they have even become dupes to all the pretended charms, necromances, amulets, and divinations of the blinded negroes, and put more trust in such things than the wiser sort among the natives. A part of this spirit of infatuation was growing upon me; in time perhaps I might have yielded to the whole: I entered into closer engagements with the inhabitants, and should have lived and died a wretch amongst them if the Lord had not watched over me for good. Not that I had lost those ideas which chiefly engaged my heart to England; but despair of seeing them accomplished, made me willing to remain where I was. I thought I could more easily bear the disappointment in this situation, than nearer home. But, as soon as I had fixed my connections and plans with these views, the Lord providentially interposed to break them in pieces, and save me from ruin in spite of myself."

By this time, the ship which had orders to take him home, arrived at Sierra, and the captain made inquiries for him there, and at the Benanoes; but understanding that he was at a great distance in the country, he thought no more about him. Had this vessel sailed without him, he would probably have become engrossed in business, to the forgetfulness of every thing else; and might have spent the greater part, or the whole of his life, in the detestable occupation of a slave-dealer. But he was rescued from this situation, by a remarkable concurrence of circumstances, which he thus describes:

"Without doubt the hand of God directed my being placed at Kittam just at this time, for, as the ship came no nearer than the Benanoes, and staid but a few days, if I had been at the Plantanes, I could not perhaps have heard of her till she had been sailed. The same must have certainly been the event, had I been sent to any other factory, of which my new master had several upon different rivers. But though the place I was at, was a long way up a river, much more than a hundred miles distant from the Plantanes, yet, by the peculiar situation which I have already noticed, I was still within a mile of the sea coast. To make the interposition more remarkable, I was, at that very juncture, going in quest of trade to a place at some distance directly from the sea, and should have set out a day or two before, but that we waited for a few articles from the next ship that offered, to complete the assortment of goods I was to take with me. We used sometimes to walk to the beach, in expectation of seeing a vessel pass by; but this was very precarious, as, at that time, the place was not at all resorted to by ships for trade. Many passed in the night,

others kept at a considerable distance from
the shore. In a word, I do not know that any
one had stopped while I was there, though
some had before, upon observing a signal
made from the shore. In February 1747, (I
know not the exact day,) my fellow servant
walking down to the beach in the forenoon,
saw a vessel sailing past, and made a smoke
in token of trade. She was already a little
beyond the place, and, as the wind was fair,
the captain was in some demur whether to
stop or not : however, had my companion been
half an hour later, she would have gone beyond recal ; but he soon saw her come to an-
chor, and went on board in a canoe : and this
proved the ship I have spoken of. One of the
first questions he was asked, was concerning
me ; and when the captain understood I was
so near, he came on shore to deliver his message. Had an invitation from home reached
me when I was sick and starving at the Plantanes, I should have received it as life from
the dead ; but now, for the reasons already
given, I heard it, at first, with indifference.
The captain, unwilling to lose me, told a story
altogether of his own framing : he gave me a

very plausible account, how he had missed a large packet of letters and papers, which he should have brought with him; but this, he said he was sure of, having had it from my father's own mouth, as well as from his employer, that a person lately dead, had left me £400 per annum; adding further, that if I was any way embarrassed in my circumstances, he had express orders to redeem me, though it should cost one half of his cargo. Every particular of this was false; nor could I myself believe what he said about the estate; but, as I had some expectations from an aged relation, I thought a part of it might be true. But I was not long in suspense: for though my father's care and desire to see me had too little weight with me, and would have been insufficient to make me quit my retreat, yet the remembrance of Mrs. N*****, the hopes of seeing her, and the possibility, that accepting this offer might once more put me in a way of gaining her hand, prevailed over all other considerations. The captain further promised (and in this he kept his word,) that I should lodge in his cabin, dine at his table, and be his constant companion, without expecting any service from me. And thus I was suddenly freed from a captivity of about fifteen months. I had neither a thought nor a desire of this change one hour before it took place. I embarked with him, and in a few hours lost sight of Kittam.

"How much is their blindness to be pitied, who can see nothing but chance in events of this sort! So blind and stupid was I at that time, I made no reflection. I sought no direction in what had happened; like a wave of the sea driven with the wind, and tossed, I was governed by present appearances and looked no further. But he, who is eyes to the blind, was leading me in a way that I knew not."

CHAPTER IV.

Newton's situation was now very much improved, and he had the opportunity of repairing his past errors; but he was not disposed to avail himself of it. On the contrary, he seemed bent upon evil, and rejected the good that was offered him. The ship he was now in, as a passenger, was on a trading voyage, for gold, ivory, dye-wood, and beeswax; which required that she should remain a long time upon the coast. She had been five months in Africa, when he went on board; and she continued there about a year afterwards.

During this time, he had no business to engage his attention, but sometimes amused himself with studying mathematics. Except this, he says, his whole life, when awake, was a course of impiety, and profaneness. His aim appeared to be to see how far he could go in profanity; and, not content with the common oaths, he daily invented new ones; so that he was often reproved by the captain, who was, himself, a very passionate man, and not at all circumspect in his expressions. From the account he at times gave the captain of his past adventures, and from his conduct during the voyage, the captain would often say that he had a Jonah on board, for whose sake a curse attended him wherever he went; and to this cause he attributed all the troubles he afterwards met with in the course of the voyage.

On one occasion, he was very near losing his life. Though not addicted to intemperance himself, he used sometimes to promote it in others for his amusement, and even join in it. On the occasion referred to, while lying on the coast of Africa, he proposed, one evening, to the sailors to have a drinking-bout, for which he supplied the liquor, and a party of four or five, including himself, sat down upon deck to see who could hold out longest in drinking gin and rum alternately. A large sea-shell supplied the place of a glass. He began, and gave the first toast, which was an imprecation against the one who should start first. This proved to be himself. His brain was soon fired; he arose, and danced about the deck like a madman; and while he was thus diverting his companions, his hat went overboard. By the light of the moon, he saw the ship's boat, and eagerly threw himself over the side to get into her, that he might recover his hat. But his sight had deceived him; for the boat was not within his reach, as he thought, but at some distance from the ship's side. He was, however, half overboard, and would the next moment have plunged into the water, when some one caught hold of his clothes behind, and pulled him back. Thus he narrowly escaped drowning, for he could not swim, even when sober; the tide ran very strong, and all the ship's crew, except his drunken companions, were asleep.

At another time, he was exposed to great danger in an expedition he made into the woods, in search of a buffalo, which had been shot. He had undertaken to conduct a party to the spot, but missed the way. After wandering about a long time, night came on, and they were in great danger from the wild beasts which abound in that country. But, after spending a most uncomfortable night, they got back to their vessel unhurt, though suffering greatly from fear and fatigue.

At length, their business being finished, they left the coast of Africa, to return to England, about the beginning of January 1748. The voyage, as far as the banks of Newfoundland, was without any particular incident. On these banks they remained a short time, to fish for cod, principally for diversion, and left this place on the first of March, with a severe gale of wind from the west, which carried them fast homewards. By this time, the ship, which had been a long time from port, was a good deal out of repair; the sails and cordage were much worn, and altogether, she was unfit to support stormy weather. In this situation, they encountered a violent tempest on the tenth of the same month.

That night, Newton went to bed, with his usual security; but was awakened from a sound sleep, by the force of a violent sea, which broke on board the ship, so that the water forced its way below, into the cabin where he lay. This alarm was followed by a cry from the deck that the ship was sinking. As soon as he could recover himself, he attempted to go upon deck, but was met in the stairway by the captain, who desired him to bring a knife with him. While he returned for the knife, another person went up in his place, and was instantly washed overboard. They had no leisure to lament him, nor did they expect to survive him long, for the ship was found to be fast filling with water. The sea had torn away the timbers on one side, and she was already a mere wreck. They had immediate recourse to the pumps, but the water gained fast upon them. Some were set to baling in another part of the vessel; but there were only eleven or twelve to sustain this service; and, notwithstanding all they could do, the ship was nearly full of water. Had it been a common cargo, she must then have sunk; but there was a great quantity of bees wax and wood on board, which, being lighter than the water, kept the vessel up, and she, therefore, continued afloat; so that they could employ some means for their safety, which succeeded beyond their hope. In about an hour's time, the day began to dawn, and the wind abated. The crew then employed most of their clothes and bedding to stop the leaks; nailing over them pieces of boards, and at last, they found, to their great joy, that the water began to diminish.

In the beginning of this hurry, Newton was little affected: he pumped hard, and endeavoured to animate himself, and his companions. He told one of them, that, after a few days, this distress would do to talk of, over a glass of wine; but the man replied, in tears, "no, it is too late now." At one time, after making some arrangement, he said, almost without meaning, " If this will not do, the Lord have mercy upon us." Immediately, this ejaculation, the first of the kind he had uttered for years, struck him forcibly; and he asked himself, " what mercy could there be for him?" But he could not then follow up the reflection: he was obliged to return to the pump, and continued there till noon, lashed fast with ropes, that he might not be washed away by the waves, which were constantly breaking over him.

The whole day, they continued in great peril, and had to keep the pumps constantly going; so that all the crew were nearly exhausted. But towards evening the ship was freed from water, and there arose a gleam of hope. The wind was now moderate, and fair; they were moving toward their port, and they began to recover from their consternation, though still in a very alarming situation. They found, that the water having floated all moveable things in the hold, all the casks of provisions had been beaten to pieces by the violent motion of the ship. The poultry and other live stock had been washed overboard, and all the provisions they had saved, except the fish they had caught on the banks, would scarcely support them a week on short allowance. The sails, too, were mostly blown away, so that they advanced but slowly, even when the wind was fair: and they were yet more than three hundred miles from land; so that they had still great cause for fear.

Things continued thus for four or five days when they were awakened, one morning, by the joyful cry of the watch on deck, of "land ho! land ho!" They were all soon aroused. It was just day-break; the dawning was uncommonly beautiful, and they were presented with a most gladdening prospect. It seemed a mountainous coast about twenty miles off, terminating in a cape; and, a little further, two or three small islands, or hummocks, as if just rising out of the water. The appearance and position seemed exactly answering to their hopes; resembling the north-west extremity of Ireland, for which they were steering. They congratulated each other, in full confidence, that, if the wind continued fair, they should soon be in safety, and plenty : and in this belief, they drank what little brandy they had left, and eat up the residue of their bread. But while they were thus rejoicing, the mate said in a grave tone, "he wished it might prove land at last." If one of the common sailors had said this, he would probably have been beaten for raising such an unreasonable doubt. It brought on, however, warm debates whether it was land or not; which were soon decided without any doubt in the negative; for the day was advancing fast, and in a little time one of the fancied islands began to grow red from the approach of the sun, which soon arose just under it. They were then convinced they had been too prodigal of their bread; the supposed land was nothing but clouds; and in half an hour more, the whole appearance was dissipated.

This was a sad disappointment. However, they comforted themselves, that though they could not yet see land, they soon would; the wind hitherto continuing favourable. But in this also they were disappointed. That very day, the fair wind subsided, and the next day, the gales sprung up from the opposite direction; and continued so for more than a fortnight afterwards. Besides, the ship was so wrecked, that they sailed to great disadvantage, and were driven far out of the course.

Provisions now began to fall very short, so that, though there was plenty of water, half a salted cod was a day's allowance for twelve people: they had no bread, and scarcely any clothes; which they felt the more as the weather was very cold. It required incessant labour at the pumps to keep the ship afloat; and one of their number sunk under the fatigue. But, after remaining in this condition, till they almost gave up all hope, they, at last, saw land; and, on the eighth of April, just four weeks after the storm which injured the vessel so much, they entered Lough Swilly, a port in the north of Ireland, with the last of their provisions boiling in the pot, and in such a shattered condition that they must, in all human probability, have perished, had they encountered the gale, which began to blow about two hours after they were in port.

This was a most important æra in Newton's life. It was in the midst of these scenes of danger and privation, that he was brought to serious reflection upon his past life; and a thorough change was wrought in his character. In his account of himself, at this time, he says, "I had many outward hardships to struggle with. The straits of hunger, cold, weariness, and the fears of sinking, and starving, I shared in common with others; but besides these, I felt a heart-bitterness, which was properly my own; no one on board, but myself, being impressed with any sense of the hand of God in our danger and deliverance, at least not awakened to any concern for their souls. No temporal dispensations can reach the heart, unless the Lord himself applies them. My companions in danger were either quite unaffected, or soon forgot it all; but it was not so with me: not that I was any wiser or better than they, but because the Lord was pleased to vouchsafe me peculiar mercy, otherwise I was the most unlikely person in the ship to receive an impression, having been often before quite stupid and hardened in the very face of great dangers, and always to this time had hardened my neck still more and more after every reproof. I can see no reason why the Lord singled me out for mercy, but this, 'that so it seemed good to him;' unless it was to show, by one astonishing instance, that with him 'nothing is impossible.'

"There were no persons on board to whom I could open myself with freedom, concerning the state of my soul, none from whom I could ask advice. As to books, I had a New Testament, Stanhope, already mentioned, and a volume of bishop Beveridge's sermons, one of which, upon our Lord's passion, affected me much. In perusing the New Testament, I was struck with several passages, particularly that of the fig-tree, Luke xiii. The case of St. Paul, 1 Tim. i. but particularly the prodigal, Luke xv. a case, I thought, that had never been so nearly exemplified, as by myself; and then the goodness of the father in receiving, nay, in running to meet such a son, and this, intended only to illustrate the Lord's goodness to returning sinners,—this gained upon me. I continued much in prayer; I saw that the Lord had interposed so far to save me, and I hoped he would do more. The outward circumstances helped in this place to make me still more serious and earnest in crying to him, who alone could relieve me; and sometimes I thought I could be content to die, even for want of food, so I might but die a believer. Thus far I was answered, that before we arrived in Ireland, I had a satisfactory evidence in my own mind of the truth of the gospel, as considered in itself, and its exact suitableness to answer all my needs. I saw that, by the way there pointed out, God might declare, not his mercy only, but his justice also, in the pardon of sin, on the account of the obedience and sufferings of

Jesus Christ. My judgment, at that time, embraced the sublime doctrine of 'God manifest in the flesh, reconciling the world to himself.' I had no idea of those systems which allow the Saviour no higher honour than that of an upper servant, or, at the most, a demigod. I stood in need of an Almighty Saviour, and such a one I found described in the New Testament. Thus far, the Lord had wrought a marvellous thing: I was no longer an infidel; I heartily renounced my former profaneness, and I had taken up some right notions, was seriously disposed, and sincerely touched with a sense of the undeserved mercy I had received, in being brought safe through so many dangers. I was sorry for my mis-spent life, and purposed an immediate reformation: I was quite freed from the habit of swearing, which seemed to have been deeply rooted in me, as a second nature. Thus, to all appearance, I was a new man."

While the ship was refitting at Lough Swilly, Newton went to Londonderry; which is on the coast of Ireland nearest to England.

He was now a serious professor of religion; attended strictly to all his religious duties, and embraced the first opportunity of making a public profession of his faith.

CHAPTER V

DURING his stay in Ireland, Newton wrote home to inform his friends of his arrival. The vessel he was in, had not been heard of for eighteen months, and had been given up for lost; so that his father had no expectation of ever seeing or hearing from him again: but he received his son's letter a few days before he left London. He was just going out governor of York Fort, in Hudson's Bay, whence he never returned. Before going, however, he paid a visit to his son's friends in Kent, and gave his consent to the marriage which had been long talked of.

Newton did not arrive in England until after his father's departure. He was, however, very kindly received by Mr. Manesty, the gentleman whose ship had brought him home, and who always afterwards took great interest in his welfare. This friend immediately offered him the command of a ship; which, upon mature consideration, he declined for the present. He prudently reflected that he had always been unsettled, and careless, and therefore thought he had better make another voyage first, that he might learn to obey, and acquire more experience of business, before he ventured to undertake such a charge. The mate of the vessel he had come home in, was appointed to the command of a new ship, and Newton engaged to go, as mate, with him.

His business, in this voyage, while on the coast, was, to sail from place to place, in the long boat, and purchase slaves. The ship was at Sierra Leone, and he was at the Plantanes, the scene of his former captivity, when he was attacked with a violent fever. During this illness, he suffered great distress of mind, from a sense of his extreme sinfulness, and of his ingratitude for mercies received; which led him to deeper repentance, and renewed and strengthened his pious resolutions.

His leisure hours, in this voyage, were chiefly employed in learning Latin, which he had entirely forgotten. He was led to this, by an imitation of one of Horace's odes, he met with in a magazine. He had no dictionary, and his only aids were, an old English translation of Horace, and a Latin Bible, which he happened to have. With the assistance of these, and by dint of close industry, he made some progress; so that, he not only understood most of the odes, and some of the Epistles; but began to relish the beauties of the composition.

His business in the long-boat, during eight months he was upon the coast, exposed him to innumerable perils, from burning suns, and chilling dews, winds, rains, and thunder storms, in the open boat: and, on shore, from long journeys through the woods, and the temper of the natives, who were frequently cruel and treacherous. Several boats were, during that time, cut off; several white men poisoned; and, of his own crew he buried six or seven people, from fevers. When going to the shore, or returning from it, in a small boat, he was several times overset by the violence of the surf, and nearly lost, as he could not swim. One escape he mentions particularly, as worthy of notice.

" When our trade was finished, and we were near sailing to the West Indies, the only remaining service I had to perform in the boat, was to assist in bringing the wood and water from the shore. We were then at Rio Cestors. I used to go into the river in the afternoon, with the sea breeze, procure my loading in the evening, and return on board in the morning, with the land wind. Several of these little voyages I had made; but the boat was grown old, and almost unfit for use. This service likewise was almost completed. One day, having dined on board, I was preparing to return to the river, as formerly; I had taken leave of the captain, received his orders, was ready in the boat, and just going to put off, as we term it; that is, to let go our ropes, and sail from the ship. In that instant, the captain came up from the cabin, and called me on board again. I went, expecting further orders; but he said he had "taken it in his head" (as he phrased it,) that I should remain that day in the ship, and accordingly ordered another man to go in my room. I was surprised at this, as the boat had never been sent away without me before, and asked him the reason. He could give me no reason, but as above, that so he would have it. Accordingly, the boat went without me, but returned no more. She sunk that night in the river, and the person who had supplied my place was drowned. I was much struck when we received news of the event the next morning. The captain himself, though quite a stranger to religion, so far as to deny a particular providence, could not help being affected; but he declared, that he had no other reason for countermanding me at that time, but that it came suddenly into his mind to detain me."

A few days after this occurrence, they sailed for Antigua, an island in the West Indies, and thence to Charleston, in South Carolina, where they remained some time, and then returned to Liverpool. When the ship's affairs were settled, Newton went to London, and, soon after, proceeded to Kent. More than seven years had now elapsed, since his first visit. No views of the kind could have appeared more chimerical, or have existed under greater discouragements, than his had done. But, in that time, great changes, both in his character, and circumstances, had taken place. Every obstacle was now removed.

He had renounced his former follies; his interest was established; and, friends on all sides agreeing, he gained the young lady's consent, without any great difficulty, and they were married, on the first of February 1750.

This marriage seems to have been in every respect a happy one; they lived long together, with many vicissitudes in outward circumstances, but with unabated affection: and, speaking of his wife, after her death, he says, "She was my pleasing companion, my " most affectionate friend, my judicious coun- " seller. I seldom or ever repented of acting " according to her advice. And I seldom act- " ed against it, without being convinced, by " the event, that I was wrong."

CHAPTER VI.

After his marriage, Mr. Newton remained a few months in the enjoyment of domestic happiness; but, in June, received orders to repair to Liverpool, to take command of a new ship in the African trade, in which he sailed from that port, in the month of August 1750. He was thus placed in a highly responsible station, with the charge of a large crew consisting of thirty persons, whom he endeavoured to treat well, and instruct both by example and by precept; establishing public worship, according to the liturgy of the church of England, twice every Sunday, and officiating himself.

Having now much leisure, he prosecuted the study of Latin with considerable success. He had taken care to bring a dictionary this voyage, and two or three other books. These happened to be among the most difficult of the classical authors, and required hard study to understand them. But he succeeded by perseverance, and was soon enabled to read most Latin books with tolerable ease. Finding, however, that this pursuit engrossed too much of his attention, he restrained his inclination for the classics, and devoted more of his time to religious reading.

While on the coast of Africa, this time, he received a visit from his former black mistress, with whom he had lived at the Plantanes. His circumstances had greatly improved, but the recollection of the past produced no ill will on his part. On the contrary he treated her with the greatest complaisance, and kindness; and endeavoured, by this conduct, to make her sorry for her former ill treatment of him. He had several such occasions, of taking the noblest kind of revenge, upon persons who had once despised him, and used him badly.

This voyage lasted fourteen months, during which nothing very remarkable occurred, and he returned home November 2d, 1751.

After remaining about eight months ashore, the season for business returned; and he sailed again, for the coast of Africa, in July 1752. In this part of his narrative he says, " A seafaring life is necessarily excluded from the benefit of public ordinances and christian communion; but, as I have observed, my loss upon these heads was at this time but small. In other respects, I know not any calling that seems more favourable, or affords greater advantages to an awakened mind, for promoting the life of God in the soul; especially to a person who has the command of a ship, and thereby has it in his power to restrain gross irregularities in others, and to dispose of his own time; and still more so in African voyages, as these ships carry a double proportion of men and officers to most others, which made my department very easy; and, excepting the hurry of trade, &c. upon the coast, which is rather occasional than constant, afforded me abundance of leisure. To be at sea, in these circumstances, withdrawn out of the reach of innumerable temptations, with opportunity and a turn of mind disposed to observe the wonders of God in the great deep, with the two noblest objects of sight, the expanded heavens, and the expanded ocean, continually in view; and where evident interpositions of Divine Providence, in answer to prayer, occur almost every day; these are helps to quicken and confirm the life of faith, which, in a good measure, supply to a religious sailor the want of those advantages which can be only enjoyed upon the shore. And, indeed, though my knowledge of spiritual things (as knowledge is usually estimated) was, at this time, very small, yet I sometimes look back with regret upon those scenes. I never knew sweeter or more frequent hours of divine communion than in my two last voyages to Guinea, when I was either almost secluded from society on ship-board, or when on shore among the natives. I have wandered through the woods, reflecting on the singular goodness of the Lord to me, in a place, where, perhaps, there was not a person who knew him for some thousand miles round me."

In the course of this voyage, he was exposed to great difficulties, and dangers, in the pursuit of his business. At one time, there was a conspiracy among his crew, to turn pirates, and take the ship from him; which, considering the iniquitous traffic they were engaged in, was not wonderful. But when the plot was nearly ripe, two of those concerned in it, were taken ill, and one of them died. This suspended the affair, and opened the way to its discovery. The slaves on board were, also, frequently plotting insurrections, and were sometimes on the very brink of mischief; but it was always discovered in time to be prevented.

His stay upon the coast, this voyage, was long, and the trade was very hazardous, but he escaped without injury. After completing his cargo, he sailed for the island of St. Christopher. Here, he expected to have found letters from Mrs. Newton, but was disappointed; and, under the belief that nothing but her death, or severe sickness could have prevented her writing, his uneasiness was so great, as to bring on a serious indisposition. From this, he was happily relieved by receiving several letters from her, which had been sent to the island of Antigua. And in August 1753, he returned to Liverpool, after an absence of thirteen months.

During his voyages, he wrote very frequently to Mrs. Newton, and as opportunities of sending his letters, occurred but seldom, he used to write, at stated times, so as to have several to send at once. These letters express great piety, and ardent attachment to his wife. Two or three may serve as a specimen. One is dated at sea—

November 10, 1752.

"I have been walking the deck very pleasantly. It is my watch, for the ship is under sail. These silent night hours, when the weather is fair, are, to me, the most agreeable part of the voyage: for in the day time, the heat of the sun, the smoke of the furnace, and the hurry of trade, are a little troublesome; I mean, they would be so, did not the thoughts of you interpose to enliven the scene. But when the sun is set, the fires out, and all but the watch are asleep, I can enjoy myself without disturbance. I have a set of favourite themes to muse upon, which are always at hand, and cannot be easily exhausted. Sometimes, I ruminate upon what is past; at others, anticipate what I hope is to come. And sometimes, I look round me, and reflect how God has been pleased to distinguish me, in his providence, not only from the crowds, whose miseries and sufferings are obvious, but even from the most of those who suppose themselves, and would persuade others, that they are happy. But so scanty are the general notions of earthly happiness, compared with mine, that I doubt not, there are thousands in possession of great outward advantages, who yet, in their brightest intervals, never felt half of the satisfaction, which at this moment warms my heart; though now it is a time of trial and exercise with me, being removed, a third of the globe, from the only treasure I have or wish for, upon the surface of it.

"It is now a twelvemonth since we met, after the long absence of my last voyage. The recollection of that hour, gives me a pleasure, which neither time nor distance can impair. And when I reflect, that I may hope, by the blessing of God, to be favoured with such another, I can smile at all the little incidental difficulties that may stand between us. Not that I have reason to think so highly of that one particular day; it has only the merit of being an introduction to the many which followed. For when I am with you, I know little difference of days, except between the first, and the last. These are very different indeed!"

Again, when on the coast of Africa, he wrote one dated,

Cape Mount, November 20.

"It has been out of my power to write of late. A part of the time, I was on shore, and the rest, indispensably engaged. But my prayers and warmest affection for you have found a place in every waking hour. I have made no great progress in trade as yet, but as I am in good health, and mercifully preserved from heavy troubles, I am content and thankful; and doubt not of doing well at last, by the blessing of him, who has been with me hitherto. Were I master of the whole coast of Africa, I would part with it, to procure you the same ground, and degree of peace, which I possess myself; and I am willing to hope, that you are, by this time, not far, if at all behind me: for if you seek in the path I recommend to you, I am as sure you will find it, as I am that it is to be found no where else. Were I to confine my thoughts to the dark side of human life, and reckon up, not only the evils attendant on my present situation, but the numberless calamities to which the smoothest state, on this side the grave, is exposed, I should be always in fear, both for you and myself. But when I consider that the Most High is on our side, that he is all-sufficient—that we have already had innumerable proofs of his goodness to us—and that his promise runs, to him that hath shall be given—then every disagreeable prospect vanishes."

There is another letter, written on Christmas day 1752, as follows:

Cape Mount, December 25.

" I now sit down to wish you a happy Christmas; a merry one, is a frequent phrase, but that falls far short of my desire. For I have often found mirth and happiness to be two very different things; and that either of them, when prevalent in a great degree, is inconsistent with the other. My heart is warm with the recollection of many endeared hours passed with you, when my happiness has been, for the time, complete, and yet I have not then felt the least inclination to be merry; and I have often been forced into a laugh when I have not been pleased.

" This has been a serious day with me, and after what I have written already, I need not attempt to say how much you have been concerned in it. It grieves me to think, that this is usually a season of festivity and dissipation. Surely they who think proper to notice it at all, should show their attention in a different manner. If we are really christians, and do indeed believe the tenor of the scriptures, with what serious thankfulness and joyful composure ought we to commemorate the coming of a Saviour into the world? If the little good offices we perform to each other demand a grateful return, what do we owe to him, who, of his own free motion and goodness, humbled himself so far, and suffered so much, to redeem us from extreme and endless misery? Oh! my dearest M. it is a most certain truth, that if he had not pitied us, we must have been for ever wretched. And if we continue to neglect him now, our misery will be aggravated by the refusal of the sure and only means of relief. And, however a round and series of what the world miscalls pleasure, may stifle uneasy thoughts for a time, they will at length awake, to the confusion of all who despise this mercy, and die impenitent. My subject has almost made me forget I am writing to you. For, blessed be God, I hope we are not like them. I trust we both desire to be wise in time, and to apply to the giver of all grace for that sufficiency which of ourselves we cannot attain. And if we ask we undoubtedly shall succeed. This hope fills my mouth with praise, since I now see a plain and secure path to eternal happiness not for myself only, but for you likewise, whose welfare, if I mistake not, is little less dear to me than that of my own soul. I find, as Solomon says, that love is stronger than death : for my regard for you often leads my views beyond the grave, and alleviates the thought, that we must sooner or later be separated here, with the prospect of being joined hereafter upon much preferable terms ; where our love will be refined and ennobled, and the consciousness of our being mutually and for ever happy, will fill us with a joy of which we have no present conception ; and yet, perhaps this joy will be among the least in that happy state."

It is surprising, that the man, who felt and wrote thus, could be engaged in the most abominable trade that ever disgraced mankind. But such is the force of early education. The efforts of Clarkson and Wilberforce had not, then, been exerted to direct public attention to the shocking barbarities of this vile traffic. Public sentiment was in its favour, and men of the highest character were engaged in it; and so much are men blinded by interest, that it was many years, before the people of England could be convinced of its atrocity ; and still longer, before the government could be prevailed on to abolish it.

Educated with such impressions, we are not to wonder, that Newton engaged in this business, without scruple. It was accounted a very genteel employment, and was generally a profitable one ; though it did not prove so to him. He felt his situation, as a jailor, unpleasant ; and was, sometimes, shocked with an employment, that was perpetually conversant with chains, bolts, and shackles ; but during all the time he was engaged in the slave-trade, he never had the least doubt of its lawfulness.

In a letter to his wife dated Mana, (on the coast of Africa,) January 26, 1753, he says, "Though to be absent from you is the chief part of my trial, it is not the whole. In this unhappy country I am in the midst of scenes, not only inferior, but opposite, to those which are inseparable from your company. But from being among a people who are so far from possessing such mercies as I am favoured with, that they are unable to form a conception of them, I may learn a lesson of gratitude; since the least pleasing part of my life is such, as still to leave me room to pity millions of my fellow-creatures. The three greatest blessings of which human nature is capable, are, undoubtedly, religion, liberty, and love. In each of these, how highly has God distinguished me! But here, are whole nations around me, whose languages are entirely different from each other, yet I believe they all agree in this, that they have no words among them expressive of these engaging ideas: from whence I infer, that the ideas themselves have no place in their minds. And as there is no medium between light and darkness, these poor creatures are not only strangers to the advantages which I enjoy, but are plunged in all the contrary evils. Instead of the present blessings, and bright future prospects of christianity, they are deceived and harassed by necromancy, magic, and all the train of superstitions that fear, combined with ignorance, can produce in the human mind. The only liberty of which they have any notion, is an exemption from being sold; and even from this very few are prefectly secure, that it shall not, some time or other, be their lot: for it often happens, that the man who sells another on board a ship, is himself bought and sold, in the same manner, and perhaps in the same vessel, before the week is ended."

It is, however, but justice to his character to add, that his sentiments on this subject were altogether changed; and when publishing the above letter, in the latter part of his life, he annexed to it, the following note.

" The reader may perhaps wonder, as I now do myself, that knowing the state of this vile traffic to be as I have here described, and abounding with enormities which I have not mentioned, I did not, at the time, start with horror at my own employment, as an agent in promoting it. Custom, example, and interest, had blinded my eyes. I did it ignorantly; for I am sure, had I thought of the slave-trade then, as I have thought of it since, no considerations would have induced me to continue in it. Though my religious views were not very clear, my conscience was very tender, and I durst not have displeased God, by acting against the light of my mind. Indeed, a slave-ship, while upon the coast, is exposed to such innumerable and continual dangers, that I was often then, and still am, astonished that any one, much more so many, should leave the coast in safety. I was then favoured with an uncommon degree of dependance upon the providence of God, which supported me; but this confidence must have failed in a moment, and I should have been overwhelmed with distress and terror if I had known or even suspected that I was acting wrong. I felt the disagreeableness of the business very strongly. The office of a jailor, and the restraints under which I was forced to keep my prisoners, were not suitable to my feelings; but I considered it as the line of life which God in his providence had allotted me, and as a cross which I ought to bear with patience and thankfulness, till he should be pleased to deliver me from it. Till then, I only thought myself bound to treat the slaves under my care with gentleness, and to consult their ease and convenience, as far as was consistent with the safety of the whole family, of whites and blacks, on board my ship."

How gratifying to the friends of humanity

to know that this change of sentiment has become universal; and that the iniquitous traffic in human flesh, is now regarded with the horror it deserves! After many years of incessant exertion, the friends of abolition succeeded in England; and, as soon as permitted by the constitution, the Congress of the United States forbad the prosecution of the slave-trade under very severe penalties. But still avarice triumphed, and notwithstanding the law declares it piracy, and punishes all concerned in it with death; men have been found, bold enough, and wicked enough, to continue the trade, almost as openly as before. Although forbidden by the laws of most christian countries, it is supposed that the slave-trade is carried on almost as extensively as ever; and that more than one hundred thousand slaves are still annually taken from the coast of Africa.

Among the many remedies which have been suggested for this evil, the only one which seems likely to produce much effect, is that of planting colonies upon the coast of Africa, for the double purpose, of cutting off the slave dealers from intercourse with the

Part of Regentstown, in the colony of Sierra Leone.

interior; and of instructing the natives in the arts of civilized life.

The English colony at Sierra Leone, though founded with the most benevolent views, failed of its object, from the defects in its organization. The American Colonization Society have attempted one on a different plan, and thus far, their efforts have been crowned with success. In 1821, they purchased a tract of land, and laid out a town at the mouth of the Messurado river; the very centre of that region which Newton and his companions visited for the purpose of procuring slaves. After overcoming the difficulties, necessarily incident to the first settlement, in such a situation, the colony has been constantly improving in its condition, and is now a flourishing community, comprising two thousand inhabitants, besides the natives who have placed themselves under its protection. The territory of the colony, purchased from the natives, and called Liberia, extends about one hundred and fifty miles along the coast, and this whole district, which was formerly the resort of slave dealers, and the scene of the most atrocious cruelties, is now the peaceful

a. The principal settlement at the Cape.   b. Round Tower or Stockton Castle.   c. Thompson's town, an establishment for Africans recaptured from slave ships.

abode of freemen. The factories of the slave-traders, which abounded there, have been destroyed, and now, not one is to be found within the limits of Liberia.

The colonial government, too, by its justice and kindness toward the native tribes, has acquired their respect and confidence; so that many have placed themselves under its protection. Numbers of the native children are sent into the colony to be educated, and a beneficial influence is exerted by the inducements offered to the neighbouring tribes to engage in useful occupations.

A full account of the colony of Liberia, would be inconsistent with the plan of this memoir; but this short digression may serve to direct attention to this interesting subject.

CHAPTER VII.

AFTER a short stay, of but six weeks, at home, Mr. Newton commenced his third, and last voyage to Africa. Just before he went, he met with a young man, whom he had formerly known on board the Harwich; and whose history is a warning lesson to all, who exert their influence to corrupt their companions. Newton gives the following account of him.

" Before I sailed, I met with a young man, who had formerly been a midshipman and my intimate companion, on board the Harwich. He was, at the time I first knew him, a sober youth, but I found too much success in my unhappy attempts to infect him with libertine principles. When we met at L———, our acquaintance renewed upon the ground of our former intimacy. He had good sense, and had read many books. Our conversation frequently turned upon religion, and I was desirous to repair the mischief I had done him. I gave him a plain account of the manner and reason of my change, and used every argument to persuade him to relinquish his infidel schemes; and when I sometimes pressed him so close, that he had no other reply to make, he would remind me that I was the very first person who had given him an idea of his liberty. This occasioned me many mournful reflections. He was then going master to Guinea himself, but before his ship was ready, his merchant became a bankrupt, which disconcerted his voyage. As he had no further expectations for that year, I offered to take him with me as a companion, that he might gain a knowledge of the coast; and the gentleman who employed me, promised to provide for him upon his return. My view in this, was not so much to serve him in his business, as to have opportunity of debating the point with him at leisure; and I hoped, in the course of my voyage, my arguments, example, and prayers, might have some good effect on him. My intention in this step was better than my judgment, and I had frequent reason to repent it. He was exceedingly profane, and grew worse and worse; I saw in him a most lively picture of what I had once been, but it was very inconvenient to have it always before my eyes. Besides, he was not only deaf to my remonstrances himself, but laboured all that he could to counteract my influence upon others. His spirit and passions were likewise exceeding high, so that it required all my prudence and authority to hold him in any degree of restraint. He was as a sharp thorn in my side for some time; but at length I had an opportunity upon the coast of buying a small vessel, which I supplied with a cargo from my own, and gave him the command, and sent him away to trade on the ship's account. When we parted, I repeated and enforced my best advice. I believe his friendship and regard were as great as could be expected, where principles were so diametrically opposite. He seemed greatly affected when I left him, but my words had no weight with him. When he found himself at liberty from under my eye, he gave a hasty loose to every appetite; and his violent irregularities, joined to the heat of the climate, soon threw him into a malignant fever, which carried him off in a few days. He died convinced, but not changed. The account I had from those who were with him was dreadful; his rage and despair struck them all with horror, and he pronounced his own fatal doom before he expired, without any appearance that he either hoped or asked for mercy. I thought this awful contrast might not be improper to give you, as a stronger view of the distinguishing goodness of God to me, the chief of sinners."

After remaining about four months on the coast, Newton sailed again for St. Christopher's. During this voyage, he was attacked by a fever, which reduced him so much, that it was thought he could not recover. The following letter, written before the disease overcame him, shows his feelings on that occasion.

At Sea, April 18.

" A few days ago, I informed you that I had left Africa, in good health and spirits. It has now pleased God to give me, in my own person, an experience of that uncertainty of all human affairs, which I have so often remarked in the concerns of others.

"I have been ill three days of a fever, which, though it is at present attended with no symptoms particularly dangerous, it behooves me to consider, may terminate in death. I have endeavoured to compose myself to the summons, if it should so prove. And I hope I may say, I am in some measure ready to live or die, as may be appointed; and that I desire not to choose for myself in this case, more than in any other. One specious excuse, with which I have often covered my desire of life, was that I might have opportunity of doing something for the glory of God, and the good of my fellow-creatures; that I might not go quite useless out of the world. But alas! I have so little improved the talents and occasions, which have been already afforded me, that I am ashamed to offer this plea any more. My only remaining concern is upon your account; and even in that I am in a measure relieved, from the following considerations.

" My first and principal consolation is in the hope, that we are both under the influence of religious principles, and that you, as well as myself, are persuaded, that no trouble or change can befall us by chance. Whenever a separation shall take place, as if not now it sooner or later must, it will be by the express act and will of the same wise and good Providence, which brought us together at first; has given us so much in each other already, and has continually shielded us, as yet, from the various harms which have been fatal to many of our acquaintance. Farther I consider, that *the time is short.* If I go now, in a few years, perhaps much sooner, you will follow me, I hope in the same path, depending wholly on the divine mercy, through faith in the blood and mediation of Jesus Christ our Redeemer, according to the plain, literal terms of the gospel. It is in this faith I am now happy. This bears me in a measure, above my fears and sins, above my sickness, and above the many agreeable views I had formed in my mind, upon a happy return to you. May this be your support, your guide and shield, and I can ask no more for you. Then you will at last attain complete and unfading happiness; and we shall meet again, and, perhaps, to join in recollecting the scenes we have been engaged in together, while upon earth. Then, probably, we shall clearly see what I now believe, and from which I derive another reason for acquiescence ; that as the goodness of God first joined us, so it was his mercy that parted us again. Mercy to each, to both of us.

We have, perhaps, been sometimes too happy in each other; to have been always or longer so, might have betrayed us into a dangerous security. We might have forgotten our present duty, and our future destination. It has been too much the case already: I have greatly failed myself, and have been but a poor example for you. Should it therefore please God, to make my death the happy occasion of fixing your dependence, hope, and desire, upon him alone; surely I can say, Thy will be done. My heart bleeds when I represent to myself, the grief with which such an event would overwhelm you. But I know that he can moderate and sanctify it, and give you cause hereafter to say, it was good for you to have been so afflicted; and ere long, the time will come, when all tears shall be wiped, both from your eyes and mine."

He, however, recovered, and arrived at St. Christopher's in safety. While there, he formed an acquaintance with a pious captain of a London ship, whose conversation was very instructive, and with whom he was very much pleased. After spending a month at this island, he sailed for Liverpool, where he arrived safely, in August 1754. The following reflections on his cause for contentment with his situation, contained in a letter, written to his wife a few days before reaching England, deserve to be remembered.

" Perhaps we have sometimes been tempted to think, that because we do not possess titles and estates, and are not of high distinction and estimation in the world, we have received nothing extraordinary; but two reflections will, I hope, suffice to correct this mistake.

" Let us in the first place, think of the miseries we know or observe in the world. How many are crippled, or maimed in their bodies, or disordered in their minds! How many at this minute, are nearly perishing through extreme want of the common necessaries of life! How many are chained to their beds, by sickness and excruciating pains, and can find no ease by day or by night! not to insist upon the more deplorable case of those, who are suffering the agonies of a wounded spirit, or a terrified conscience. Let us reflect on the miseries and outrages which the scourge of war brings upon cities, provinces, and whole nations. Or, if those scenes are too shocking to dwell upon, it will suffice to take the estimate much lower. Let us look round us at home, amongst our own acquaintance, or at farthest, within the bounds of the newspapers. How many fatherless— how many widows do we hear of! How many, from happy prospects, rendered suddenly miserable, by what we call casualties! Take these things together, and let us ask our consciences, if a continued exemption from such a variety of evils, and a constant supply of the many wants we have in common with others, are not favours which we enjoy, and which are afforded, comparatively, to few?

"But farther, let us, in the second place, turn our eyes to those who are placed in the smoother walks of life, whom customary speech calls the *happy*. Run over what you know of those who are most noticed for personal qualifications, for their riches, honours, or the variety of their means and modes of pleasure: and then let us ask ourselves, if there is any one amongst all these, with whom we would be content to change in all points? If we should not accept such a proposal, as surely we should not, (I answer for you no less confidently than for myself,) it follows evidently, that we have more to be thankful for, (our own partial selves being judges,) than many of those whom, perhaps, we have been disposed to envy; and if so, it is equally plain, that there are no two persons upon the face of the earth, more indebted to an indulgent Providence than ourselves."

When Mr. Newton returned to England, this time, he was of opinion that the African business was too much overdone, to be profitable, and so advised his employer; but Mr. Manesty thought otherwise, and determined to send out another vessel very soon. Mr. Newton, therefore, expected to sail again in a very short time; and after spending a few weeks at home, he returned to Liverpool, to make the necessary preparations for his departure. These were all completed, and he was to sail in two days, when an event occurred, which deranged all his plans, and produced an entire change in his pursuits. He was sitting at tea, in the afternoon, with Mrs. Newton, apparently in as good health as usual, when he was suddenly seized with a fit, which deprived him of sense and motion, and left no other sign of life than that of breathing. This lasted about an hour; but when he recovered, it left a painful dizziness in his head, which continued, with such symptoms as induced the physicians to declare, that it would not be safe or prudent to proceed on the voyage. Accordingly, by the advice of his friend, Mr. Manesty, to whom the ship belonged, he resigned the command, the day before she sailed; and was, by this means, unexpectedly freed from the future consequences of a voyage, which proved extremely calamitous. The person who went in his stead, most of the officers, and many of the crew died; and the vessel was brought home with great difficulty.

Being thrown out of active employment Mr. Newton spent the following year chiefly in London and in Kent. During this period, he was in great anxiety on account of Mrs. Newton, who was very ill, in consequence of the shock, occasioned by his sudden indisposition. Her surprise threw her into a disorder, which seemed beyond the reach of medicine. Without any of the ordinary symptoms of consumption, she decayed almost visibly, till she became so weak, that she could hardly bear any one to walk across the room she was in. He was kept in this state of anxiety, near eleven months; and it was not till after he was settled at Liverpool, that she began to amend, and finally recovered.

In August, 1755, he was appointed Tide Surveyor at Liverpool, through the influence of his kind friend Mr. Manesty, and under circumstances somewhat curious. An unfounded report was circulated, that his immediate predecessor in the office intended to resign, in consequence of which, Mr. Manesty applied for the situation, for Mr. Newton; and the very day he received the promise of it, the incumbent was found dead in his bed, though he had been in company and in perfect health the night before. The same messenger who brought the promise, carried back the news of the vacancy. About an hour after, the Mayor applied for a nephew of his, but he was too late.

Mr. Newton was in Kent when he received information of this appointment, and was obliged to repair immediately to Liverpool, though his wife was then apparently in the last stage of her disease. This, however, was happily not the case. She began to recover, about that time, and, in October, was enabled to join him in Liverpool.

He was now comfortably situated, in an employment much better suited to his feelings than his former occupation. His office yielded him a competent maintenance, and allowed him sufficient leisure to pursue his favourite studies. He applied himself to learn Greek, so as to understand the New Testament, and the Septuagint; and, when he had made some progress in this, he commenced the study of Hebrew. His aim was, not to become a critical scholar, but to be able to read the scriptures in their original languages; and in this he succeeded. Together with these, he read some of the best writers on divinity, in Latin, English, and French; and accustomed himself to writing on these subjects. His object in these studies, was to prepare himself for the ministry, to which his attention was directed by his own feelings, and the advice of some of his friends.

From the time of his reformation, Mr. Newton was a firm believer in a particular providence; a belief which was strongly impressed upon him by many wonderful incidents in his own life. One of these occurred while he was at Liverpool. His business was, to visit and inspect vessels arriving in the port. He was remarkably punctual in all his appointments, and would, sometimes, sit with his watch in his hand, lest he should fail in keeping an engagement. One day, however, some business had so detained him, that he came to his boat much later than usual, to the surprise of those who had noticed his former punctuality. But while going out as usual, to inspect a ship, she blew up, just before he reached her; so that if he had left the shore a few minutes sooner, he must have perished with the rest on board.

In 1758, he applied to the Archbishop of York for ordination; but, notwithstanding he was recommended by the bishop of Chester, the archbishop was unwilling to relax the rules of the church in his favour, and therefore refused him on account of some difference in doctrinal views. Upon this disappointment, he was strongly inclined to join the dissenters, under a belief that it was his duty to preach; but he relinquished this purpose at the persuasion of his wife.

In 1764, the curacy of Olney was proposed to him, and he was then admitted to orders, after examination by the bishop of Lincoln, to whom his difference of opinion did not appear a sufficient objection to his admission into the established church. He was ordained Deacon, in April, 1764, and Priest, in June, the following year. He continued to reside at Olney nearly sixteen years. During this time, he devoted himself faithfully to his parochial charge, always labouring for the good of his parishioners, and zealous for the promotion of religion. The life of a country clergyman, however actively useful in its sphere, furnishes few incidents for history; and there is, therefore, little to relate of him, but that he was distinguished for his active benevolence and ardent piety. He was greatly assisted in his benevolent projects by the celebrated Mr. Thornton, who sought his acquaintance, after having read his narrative, and whose liberality always supplied him with the means of being extensively useful. Of this distinguished philanthropist, it may truly be said, that he devoted his substance to the service of God and the good of his fellow men. Possessed of immense wealth, the fruit of persevering and successful industry as a merchant, his great delight seemed to be to expend it in such a manner as to do most good. By a well-ordered economy, without the least meanness in his personal expenses, he secured the means of employing a considerable part of his wealth in promoting the happiness of others. Animated by the genuine spirit of Christian charity, his whole soul was engaged in works of benevolence, from a desire to serve God and promote the best interests of man.

" Mr. Thornton was a Christian indeed; that is, he was alive to God by a spiritual regeneration. With this God he was daily and earnestly transacting that infinitely momentous affair, the salvation of his own soul; and, next to that, the salvation of the souls of others. Temperate in all things, though mean in nothing, he made provision for doing good with his opulence, and seemed to be most in his element when appropriating a considerable part of his large income to the necessities of others."

While at Olney, Mr. Newton became intimately acquainted with the poet Cowper, whose character is so interesting, from the sweetness, the piety, and the sadness of his poetry; and who came to reside at Olney, labouring under that morbid melancholy which rendered his life so miserable.

Of this acquaintance, Newton's friend and biographer says, " Providence seems to have appointed Mr. N's residence at Olney, among other reasons, for the relief of the depressed mind of the poet Cowper. There has gone forth an unfounded report, that the deplorable melancholy of Cowper was, in part, derived from his residence and connexions in that place. The fact, however, is the reverse of this; and as it may be of importance to the interests of true religion to prevent such a misrepresentation from taking root, I will present the real state of the case, as I have found it attested by the most respectable living witnesses; and more especially as confirmed by a manuscript, written by the poet himself, at the calmest period of his life, with the perusal of which I was favoured by Mr. N.

"It most evidently appears, that symptoms of Mr. Cowper's morbid state began to discover themselves in his earliest youth. He seems to have been at all times disordered, in a greater or less degree. He was sent to Westminster school at the age of nine years, and long endured the tyranny of an elder boy, of which he gives a shocking account in the paper above-mentioned; and which produced, as one of his biographers observes who had long intimacy with him, 'an indelible effect upon his mind through life.'

"Naturally fearful and depressed in his temper, he met with many disappointments in life, which cast a gloom over his mind. His own language is—

'Doomed, as I am, in solitude to waste
The present moments, and regret the past;
Deprived of every joy I valued most—
My friend torn from me, and my mistress lost—
Call not this gloom I wear, this anxious mien,
The dull effect of humour or of spleen;

" That any man, under such pressures, should at first turn his mind to those resources which religion alone can afford, is both natural and rational. But Mr. Cowper was like a person looking from a high tower, who perceives only the danger of falling, but neither the security nor prospect it presents; and therefore it is no wonder, with so melancholy, morbid, and susceptible a mind, that his unhappiness should be increased. And yet this very mind of Cowper, when put under the care of Dr. Cotton, received the first consolation it ever tasted, and that from evangelical truths. It was under the care of this physician, that Mr. Cowper first obtained a clear view of those sublime truths, which so exalted his future strains as a poet. Here also he received that settled tranquillity and peace, which he enjoyed for several years afterwards. So far, therefore, was his constitutional malady from being produced or increased by his evangelical connexions, either at St. Alban's or at Olney, that he seems never to have had any settled peace but from the truths he learned in those societies. It appears, that among them alone he found the only sunshine he ever enjoyed, through the cloudy day of his afflicted life."

Mr. Newton used to say, that he looked upon Mr. Cowper as a sort of curate or assistant minister, from his constant attendance on the sick and afflicted. He studied his bible closely, and received from it those consolations which it is designed to give.

While living together at Olney, Newton and Cowper united to prepare a volume of hymns, which were afterwards published, under the title of " Olney Hymns:" but, owing to Cowper's illness, he furnished but few in the collection. In the preface, Newton says, " the whole number were composed by two persons only. The original design would not admit of any other association. A desire of promoting the faith and comfort of sincere christians, though the principal, was not the only motive for this undertaking. It was likewise intended as a monument to perpetuate the remembrance of an intimate and endeared friendship. With this pleasing view, I entered on my part, which would have been smaller than it is, and the book would have appeared much sooner, and in a very different form, if the wise, though mysterious providence of God had not seen fit to cross my wishes. We had not proceeded far, upon our proposed plan, before my dear friend was prevented, by a long and affecting indisposition, from affording me any farther assistance. My grief and disappointment were great; I hung my harp upon the willows, and for some time thought myself determined to proceed no farther without him."

It was at Olney, too, that Newton became acquainted with Mr. Scott, the celebrated commentator on the Bible, who was then the curate of a neighbouring parish. Mr. Scott was, at that time, very unsettled in his religious principles. He was nearly a Socinian, was in the habit of ridiculing evangelical religion, and even attempted to bring Newton over to his opinions. The change which afterwards took place in his feelings, and his conversion, indeed, from a state of great looseness of sentiment, he attributed to the influence of Mr. Newton's pious example and conversation. This is one of the most interesting events in the life of Newton, and Mr.

Scott, in his own writings, does full justice to the piety and sincerity of his spiritual guide.

"In the year 1776, Mr. N. was afflicted with a tumour, or wen, which had formed on his thigh; and on account of its growing more large and troublesome, he resolved to have it cut out by a surgeon. This obliged him to go to London for the operation, which was successfully performed, October 10th, by the late Mr. Warner, of Guy's Hospital. I remember hearing him speak several years afterwards of this trying occasion; but the trial did not seem to have affected him as a painful operation, so much as a critical opportunity in which he might fail in demonstrating the patience of a Christian under pain. 'I felt,' said he, 'that being enabled to bear a very sharp operation, with tolerable calmness and confidence, was a greater favour granted to me than the deliverance from my malady.'"

In addition to his regular parochial duties he published several works. After his first application for ordination, he published some sermons, which he had intended for delivery.

In 1762, he published a series of letters on religious subjects, signed Omicron and Vigil: in 1764, his Narrative: in 1767, a volume of Sermons, preached at Olney: in 1769, a Review of Ecclesiastical History, and in 1779, a volume of Hymns, of which some were composed by Mr. Cowper. To these was afterwards added, in 1781, a series of Letters, called Cardiphonia, or the utterance of the heart.

In 1779, Mr. Newton left Olney, for the rectory of the united parishes of St. Mary Woolnoth, and St. Mary Woolchurch Haw, in London; to which he was presented by his friend Mr. Thornton.

He was now placed in an entirely new scene; in the midst of a large city, and with a new class of duties to perform. But he entered upon them, with his characteristic zeal and humility, and soon acquired the esteem and reverence of those around him. His house was always open to those who wished for advice or instruction; and he was particularly pleased to instruct and encourage the younger ministers, or candidates for the ministry. In his preaching, he always aimed at doing good; and when some of his friends observed to him that his sermons were short, he said that he made them so upon principle, as there might be some men of business in church, who had been strangers to his views of the truth, and he did not wish to disgust them, but rather to attract them.

Mr. Cecil who knew him well, and esteemed him highly, says, "Here a new and very distinct scene of action and usefulness was set before him. Placed in the centre of London, in an opulent neighbourhood, with connexions daily increasing, he had now a course of service to pursue, in several respects different from his former at Olney. Being, however, well acquainted with the word of God, and the heart of man, he proposed to himself no new weapons of warfare, for pulling down the strong-holds of sin and Satan around him. He perceived, indeed, most of his parishioners too intent upon their wealth and merchandise to pay much regard to their new minister; but, since they would not come to him, he was determined to go, as far as he could, to them; and, therefore, soon after his institution, he sent a printed address to his parishioners: he afterwards sent them another address on the usual prejudices that are taken up against the gospel. What effects these attempts had then upon them does not appear; certain it is, that these, and other acts of his ministry, will be recollected by them, when the objects of their present pursuits are forgotten or lamented.

"I have heard Mr. N. speak with great feeling on the circumstances of his last important station. 'That one,' said he, 'of the most ignorant, the most miserable, and the most abandoned of slaves, should be plucked from his forlorn state of exile on the coast of Africa, and at length be appointed minister of the parish of the first magistrate of the first city in the world—that he should there not only testify of such grace, but stand up as a singular instance and monument of it—that he should be enabled to record it in his history, preaching, and writings, to the world at large—is a fact I can contemplate with admiration, but never sufficiently estimate.' This reflection, indeed, was so present to his mind on all occasions, and in all places, that he seldom passed a single day any where, but he was found referring to the strange events, in one way or the other."

His whole conduct, both in the pulpit and in domestic life, was so pure, and so exemplary, that he was said to realize the description given by the author of the Deserted Village:

"Unskilful he to fawn, or seek for power,
By doctrines fashioned to the varying hour;
Far other aims his heart had learned to prize,
More bent to raise the wretched than to rise.
Thus to relieve the wretched was his pride,
And e'en his failings leaned to virtue's side;
But in his duty prompt at every call,
He watched and wept, he prayed and felt, for all:
And as a bird each fond endearment tries,
To tempt its new-fledged offspring to the skies,
He tried each art, reproved each dull delay,
Allured to brighter worlds, and led the way."

Mr. Cecil says, "there was a gentleness, a candour, and a forbearance in him, that I do not recollect to have seen in an equal degree among his brethren; and which had so conciliating an effect, that even the enemies of truth often spoke loudly in praise of his character. On the other hand it generated such an affection in his friends that, had he attempted to preach longer than he did, a great part of his congregation would have gathered, were it only for the pleasure they had in seeing his person."

His benevolence was always active, and he was always ready to do good, no matter how small the occasion. He used to say, " I see in this world two heaps of human happiness, and misery; now, if I can take but the smallest bit from one heap, and add to the other, I carry a point. If, as I go home, a child has dropped a half-penny, and, by giving it another, I can wipe away its tears, I feel I have done something. I should be glad, indeed, to do greater things, but I will not neglect this."

In the year 1784, Handel's Oratorio of the Messiah was performed in London with great applause, and, for a long time, attracted the attention of the fashionable world. This splendid musical composition is an account of the advent of the Messiah; commencing with the prophecies relating to him, then giving an account of his birth, sufferings, and death; and finally describing the glorious consummation of his undertaking, in the deliverance of his people, and their triumphant entry into heaven after the judgment of the last day: the whole set forth in deeply impressive music, and affording one of the most wonderful exhibitions of the art.

Mr. Newton thought this a good opportunity for directing the attention of his congregation in a particular manner, to the doctrine of the atonement; and he accordingly preached a course of sermons on the principal outlines of the Saviour's character, and mediation; adopting the general plan of the Oratorio, as to the order in which he treated the subject.

The fourth sermon commences with a passage, remarkable for its force and originality. The text is from Mal. iii. 1—3, " The Lord, whom ye seek, shall suddenly come to his temple," &c. and the sermon opens thus :—

" ' Whereunto shall we liken the people of this generation, and to what are they like ?' I represent to myself a number of persons, of various characters, involved in one common charge of high treason. They are already in a state of confinement, but not yet brought to their trial. The facts, however, are so plain, and the evidence against them so strong and pointed, that there is not the least doubt of their guilt being fully proved, and that nothing but a pardon can preserve them from punishment. In this situation, it should seem their wisdom to avail themselves of every expedient in their power for obtaining mercy. But they are entirely regardless of their danger, and wholly taken up with contriving methods of amusing themselves, that they may pass away the term of their imprisonment with as much cheerfulness as possible. Among other resources, they call in the assistance of music. And amidst a great variety of subjects in this way, they are particularly pleased with one. They choose to make the solemnities of their impending trial, the character of their Judge, the methods of his procedure, and the awful sentence to which they are exposed, the ground-work of a musical entertainment. And, as if they were quite unconcerned in the event, their attention is chiefly fixed upon the skill of the composer, in adapting the style of his music to the very solemn language and subject with which they are trifling. The king, however, out of his great clemency and compassion towards those who have no pity for themselves, prevents them with his goodness. Undesired by them, he sends them a gracious message. He assures them, that he is unwilling they should suffer: he requires, yea, he entreats them to submit. He points out a way in which their confession and submission shall be certainly accepted; and in this way, which he condescends to prescribe, he offers them a free and a full pardon. But instead of taking a single step towards a compliance with his goodness, they set his message likewise to music: and this, together with a description of their present state, and of the fearful doom awaiting them, if they continue obstinate, is sung for their diversion; accompanied with the sound of cornet, flute, harp, sackbut, psaltery, dulcimer, and all kinds of instruments. Surely, if such a case as I have supposed could be found in real life, though I might admire the musical taste of these people, I should commiserate their insensibility!"

In the year 1786, these sermons were published in two volumes, and the following sentiments, upon christian humility and forbearance, contained in the author's preface, well deserve to be recorded and remembered.

" From those readers, whose habits of thinking on religious subjects are formed by a close attachment to particular systems of divinity, the author requests a candid construction of what he advances, if he ventures in some instances to deviate a little from the more beaten track. If he is sometimes constrained to differ from the judgment of wise and good men, who have deserved well of the church of God, he would do it with modesty : far from depreciating their labours, he would be thankful for the benefit which he hopes he has received from them. It is a great satisfaction to him, that in all doctrinal points of primary importance, his views are confirmed by the suffrage of writers and ministers eminent for genuine piety and sound learning, who assisted him in his early inquiries after truth, and at whose feet he is still willing to sit. Yet, remembering that he is authorised and commanded to call no man master, so as to yield an implicit and unqualified submission to human teachers, while he gladly borrows every help he can from others, he ventures likewise to think for himself. His leading sentiments concerning the grand peculiarities of the gospel were formed many years since, when he was in a state of almost entire seclusion from society,—when he had scarcely any religious book but the Bible within his reach, and had no knowledge, either of the various names, parties, and opinions, by which christians were distinguished and divided, or the controversies which subsisted among them. He is not conscious that any very material difference has taken place in his sentiments since he first became acquainted with the religious world; but, after a long course of experience and observation, he seems to possess them in a different manner. The difficulties which for a season perplexed him on some points, are either removed or considerably abated. On the other hand, he now perceives difficulties that constrain him to lay his hand upon his mouth, in subjects which once appeared to him obvious and plain. Thus, if he mistakes not himself, he is less troubled with scepticism, and at the same time less disposed to be dogmatical, than he formerly was. He feels himself unable to draw the line with precision between those essential points which ought to be earnestly contended for (in a spirit of meekness,) as for the faith once delivered to the saints, and certain secondary positions, concerning which good men may safely differ, and wherein, perhaps, we cannot reasonably expect them to be unanimous during the present state of imperfection. But if the exact boundary cannot be marked with certainty, he thinks it both desirable and possible to avoid the extremes into which men of warm tempers have often been led.

" Not that the author can be an advocate for that indifference to truth, which, under the specious semblance of moderation and candour, offers a comprehension, from which none are excluded but those who profess and aim to worship God in the spirit, to rejoice in Christ Jesus, and to renounce all confidence in the flesh. Moderation is a christian grace; it differs much from that tame, unfeeling neutrality between truth and error which is so prevalent in the present day. As the different rays of light, which, when separated by a prism, exhibit the various colours of the rainbow, form, in their combination, a perfect and resplendent white, in which every colour is incorporated, so, if the graces of the Holy Spirit were complete in us, the result of their combined effects would be a truly candid, moderate, and liberal spirit towards our brethren. The christian, especially he who is advanced and established in the life of faith, has a fervent zeal for God, for the honour of his name, his law, and his gospel. The honest warmth which he feels when such a law is broken, such a gospel is despised, and when the great and glorious name of the Lord his God is profaned, would, by the occasion of his infirmities, often degenerate into anger or contempt towards those who oppose themselves, if he was under the influence of zeal only. But his zeal is blended with benevolence and humility; it is softened by a consciousness of his own frailty and fallibility. He is aware that his knowledge is very limited in itself, and very faint in its efficacy; that his attainments are weak and few compared with his deficiencies; that his gratitude is very disproportionate to his obligations, and his obedience unspeakably short of conformity to his prescribed rule; that he has nothing but what he has received, and has received nothing but what, in a greater or less degree, he has misapplied and misimproved. He is therefore a debtor to the mercy of God, and lives upon his multiplied forgiveness; and he makes the gracious conduct of the Lord towards himself, a pattern for his own conduct towards his fellow-creatures. He cannot boast; nor is he forward to censure. He considers himself, lest he also be tempted, (Gal. vi. 1;) and thus he learns tenderness and compassion to others, and to bear patiently with those mistakes, prejudices, and prepossessions in them, which once belonged to his own character, and from which, as yet, he is but imperfectly freed. But then, the same considerations which inspire him with meekness and gentleness towards those who oppose the truth, strengthen his regard for the truth itself, and his conviction of its importance. For the sake of peace, which he loves and cultivates, he accommodates himself, as far as he lawfully can, to the weakness and misapprehensions of those who mean well, though he is thereby exposed to the censure of bigots of all parties, who deem him flexible and wavering, like a reed shaken with the wind. But there are other points nearly connected with the honour of God, and essential to the life of faith, which are the foundations of his hope and the sources of his joy. For his firm attachment to these, he is content to be treated as a bigot himself; for here he is immoveable as an iron pillar, nor can either the fear or the favour of man prevail on him to give place, no not for an hour, Gal. ii. 5. Here his judgment is fixed, and he expresses it in simple and unequivocal language, so as not to leave either friends or enemies in suspense concerning the side which he has chosen, or the cause which is nearest to his heart."

In 1790, Mr. Newton suffered a severe affliction, in the loss of his wife. His attachment to her, romantic as it was in its commencement, continued unabated until her death, and the blow was proportionably severe. Her death was occasioned by a cancer in the breast; the consequence of a blow received when in Liverpool. The pain of the blow soon wore off, but it left a tumour, which she concealed from her husband as long as possible, but which gradually increased, until it was too large to be removed; and, after suffering much pain, with great fortitude, she died on the 15th December, 1790.

Although deeply afflicted by this event, he made every effort to control his feelings, and even preached her funeral sermon himself, to the surprise of those who did not know his character; but in conformity with his general rule, of submitting, implicitly, to the dispensations of Providence.

As Mr. and Mrs. Newton had no children of their own, they had adopted two nieces, who resided with them, and to whom they were very much attached. One of them died before Mrs. Newton: this was Miss Eliza Cunningham, the young lady whose biography he wrote, the simple sketch of whose character is among the most interesting of the publications of the American Sunday School Union. The other survived her, and was now the object of her uncle's tenderest affection. She was his constant companion, visited wherever he went, and when his sight failed, she read to him, divided his food, and was all to him that a dutiful daughter could be.

In 1790, the college of New Jersey in the United States, conferred upon him the honorary degree of D. D.; but he begged to decline the distinction, saying, in his reply, "I have neither the pretension nor the wish for honours of this kind."

He continued in the active performance of his ministerial duties to extreme old age; and even "when his sight was nearly gone, and he was incapable, through deafness, of joining in conversation, his public ministry was publicly continued, and maintained with a considerable degree of his former animation. His memory, indeed, was observed to fail; but his judgment in divine things still remained; and though some depression of spirits was observed, which he used to account for from his advanced age, his perception, taste, and zeal for the truths he had long received, and taught, were evident."

"After Mr. Newton was turned of eighty," says his biographer, Mr. Cecil, "some of his friends feared he might continue his public ministrations too long; they marked not only his infirmities in the pulpit, but felt much on account of the decrease of his strength, and of his occasional depressions. Conversing with him, in January 1806, on the latter, he observed, that he had experienced nothing which in the least affected the principles he had felt and taught; that his depressions were the natural result of fourscore years; and that, at any age, we can only enjoy that comfort from our principles which God is pleased to send. 'But (replied I) in the article of public preaching, might it not be best to consider your work as done, and stop before you evidently discover you can speak no longer?' 'I cannot stop,' said he, raising his voice; 'What! shall the old African blasphemer stop while he can speak?'

"In every future visit I perceived old age making rapid strides. At length his friends found some difficulty in making themselves known to him: his sight, his hearing, and his recollection exceedingly failed; but, being mercifully kept from pain, he generally appeared easy and cheerful. Whatever he uttered was perfectly consistent with the principles he had so long and so honourably maintained. Calling to see him a few days before he died, with one of his most intimate friends, we could not make him recollect either of us; but seeing him afterwards, when sitting up in his chair, I found so much intellect remaining as produced a short and affectionate reply, though he was utterly incapable of conversation.

" Mr. N. declined in this very gradual way, till at length it was painful to ask him a question, or attempt to rouse faculties almost gone; still his friends were anxious to get a word from him; and those friends who survive him will be as anxious to learn the state of his mind in his latest hours. It is quite natural thus to inquire, though it is not important, how such a decided character left this world. I have heard Mr. N. say, when he has heard particular inquiry made about the last expressions of an eminent believer, 'Tell me not how the man died, but how he lived.' "

He was fully aware of his situation, and spoke of his approaching death with perfect composure, and even joyful anticipation, to the great satisfaction of those friends who were near him. He died on the 21st of December, 1807, and was buried in the vault of his church, having left the following injunction, in a letter for the direction of his executors.

"I propose writing an epitaph for myself, if it may be put up, on a plain marble tablet, near the vestry door, to the following purport:—

JOHN NEWTON, CLERK,
Once an infidel and libertine,
A servant of slaves in Africa,
Was, by the rich mercy of our Lord and Saviour
JESUS CHRIST,
Preserved, restored, pardoned,
And appointed to preach the faith he
Had long laboured to destroy,
Near 16 years at Olney in Bucks;
And — years in this church.
On Feb. 1, 1750, he married
MARY,
Daughter of the late George Catlett,
Of Chatham, Kent.
He resigned her to the Lord who gave her
On the 15th of December 1790.

" And I earnestly desire, that no other monument, and no inscription but to this purport may be attempted for me."

We cannot better conclude this sketch of the life of this extraordinary man, than by giving the remarks with which Mr. Cecil closes his "General Observations" on the character of his departed friend.

" My dear young friends, who may have read these Memoirs, perhaps merely for your amusement, consider with what a contrary design St. Paul states his former unrenewed condition: 'I was,' says he, 'before, a blasphemer, a persecutor, and injurious; but for this cause I obtained mercy.' For what cause? Was it that men should continue in sin, because a miracle of special grace had been wrought? To ' do evil that good may come' is the black mark of a reprobate mind. But 'for this cause,' saith the apostle, 'I obtained mercy; that in me first Jesus Christ might show forth all long-suffering, for a pattern to them who should hereafter believe in him to life everlasting.' The same caution is necessary whenever you may be tempted to hope for such a recovery as Mr. N's, after erring like him. To proceed upon such a hope, is a gross presumption. Thousands perish in wrong courses, for one who escapes from their natural consequences. Pray, therefore, that you may be enabled to resist the temptation of perverting such extraordinary cases. God affords them to be 'a savour of life unto life,' while Satan would employ them to be 'a savour of death unto death.' One almighty to save affords you here, indeed, an instance of special mercy, which gives you the strongest encouragement in setting your faces towards his kingdom, and this is the proper use to be made of such a case.

" Your parents, your most disinterested friends, are anxiously watching for your good and they, perhaps, have put this book into your hand with a view of promoting it. The author has cause to thank God, who put it into the heart of his pious parent to make a similar attempt, and bless it with success; and he could tell of more such instances. May it please God that you may be added to the number! Worldly prosperity would rather hurt than help you before your minds become rightly directed. Mr. N. shows us, that his firmest friend could not have served him effectually had not God first prepared his mind for the advancement. An enemy would occupy your minds with perishing objects; but God calls you to cultivate nobler views. He proposes glory, honour, immortality, and eternal life by the gospel. 'Seek,' therefore, first the kingdom of God and his righteousness, and all other things shall be added to you.'"

REVIEW

OF

MR. NEWTON'S CHARACTER

THERE seems to be little need of giving a general character of Mr. N. after the particulars which appear in the foregoing memoirs. He unquestionably was the child of a peculiar providence, in every step of his progress; and his deep sense of the extraordinary dispensation through which he had passed, was the prominent topic in his conversation. Those who personally knew the man, could have no doubt of the probity with which his Narrative (singular as it may appear,) was written. They, however, who could not view the subject of these memoirs so nearly as his particular friends did, may wish to learn something farther of his character, with respect to his LITERARY ATTAINMENTS—his MINISTRY—his FAMILY HABITS—his WRITINGS—and his FAMILIAR CONVERSATION.

Of his LITERATURE, we learn from his narrative what he attained in the learned languages, and that by almost incredible efforts. Few men have undertaken such difficulties, under such disadvantages. It, therefore, seems more extraordinary that he should have attained so much, than that he should not have acquired more. Nor did he quit his pursuits of this kind, but in order to gain that knowledge which he deemed much more important. Whatever he conceived had a tendency to qualify him as "a scribe well instructed in the kingdom of God, bringing out of his treasury things new and old"—I say, in pursuit of this point, he might have adopted the apostle's expression, "One thing I do." By a principle so simply and firmly directed, he furnished his mind with much information: he had consulted the best old divines; had read the moderns of reputation with avidity; and was continually watching whatever might serve for analogies or illustrations, in the service of religion. "A minister," he used to say, "wherever he is, should be always in his study. He should look at every man, and at every thing, as capable of affording him some instruction.'

His mind, therefore, was ever intent on his calling—ever extracting something, even from the basest materials, which he could turn into gold.

In consequence of this incessant attention to his object, while many, whose early advantages greatly exceeded his, were found excelling Mr. N. in the knowledge and investigation of some curious abstract, but very unimportant points, he was found vastly excelling them in points of infinitely higher importance to man. In the knowledge of God, of his word, and of the human heart, in its wants and resources, Newton would have stood among mere scholars, as his name-sake, the philosopher, stood among ordinary men. I might say the same of some others who have set out late in the profession, but who, with a portion of Mr. N.'s piety and ardour, have greatly outstripped those who have had every early advantage and encouragement. Men with specious titles and high connexions have received the rewards; while men, like Newton, without them, have done the work.

With respect to his MINISTRY, he appeared, perhaps, to least advantage in the pulpit; as he did not generally aim at accuracy in the composition of his sermons, nor at any address in the delivery of them. His utterance was far from clear, and his attitudes ungraceful. He possessed, however, so much affection for his people, and zeal for their best interests, that the defect of his manner was of little consideration with his constant hearers; at the same time, his capacity, and habit of entering into their trials and experience, gave the highest interest to his ministry among them. Besides which, he frequently interspersed the most brilliant allusions, and brought forward such happy illustration of his subject, and those with so much unction on his own heart, as melted and enlarged theirs. The parent-like tenderness and affection which accompanied his instruction, made them prefer him to preachers, who, on other accounts, were much more generally popular. It ought also to be noted, that, amidst the extravagant notions, and unscriptural positions, which have sometimes disgraced the religious world, Mr. N. never departed, in any instance, from soundly and seriously promulgating the "faith once delivered to the saints," of which his writings will remain the best evidence. His doctrine was strictly that of the Church of England, urged on the consciences of men in the most practical and experimental manner. "I hope," said he one day to me, smiling, "I hope I am upon the whole a scriptural preacher: for I find I am considered as an Arminian among the high Calvinists, and as a Calvinist among the strenuous Arminians."

I never observed any thing like bigotry in his ministerial character, though he seemed at all times to appreciate the beauty of order, and its good effects in the ministry. He had formerly been intimately connected with some highly respectable ministers among the dissenters, and retained a cordial regard for many to the last. He considered the strong prejudices which attach to both churchmen and dissenters, as arising more from education than from principle. But being himself both a clergyman and an incumbent in the Church of England, he wished to be consistent. In public, therefore, he felt he could not act with some ministers, whom he thought truly good men, and to whom he cordially wished success in their endeavours; and he patiently met the consequence. They called him a bigot, and he in return prayed for them, that they might not be really such.

He had formerly taken much pains in composing his sermons, as I could perceive in one MS. which I looked through; and even latterly, I have known him, whenever he felt it necessary, produce admirable plans for the pulpit. I own I thought his judgment deficient in not deeming such preparations necessary at all times. I have sat in pain when he has spoken unguardedly in this way before young ministers: men, who, with but comparatively slight degrees of his information and experience, would draw encouragement to ascend the pulpit with but little previous study of their subject. A minister is not to be blamed, who cannot rise to qualifications which some of his brethren have attained; but he is certainly bound to improve his own talent to the utmost of his power: he is not to cover his sloth, his love of company, or his disposition to attend a wealthy patron, with the pretence of depending entirely on divine influence. Timothy had at least as good ground for expecting such influence, as any of his successors in the ministry; and yet the apostle admonishes him to "give attendance to reading, to exhortation, and to doctrine—not to neglect the gift that was in him—to meditate upon these things—to give himself wholly to them, that his profiting might appear to all."

Mr. N. regularly preached on the Sunday morning and evening at St. Mary Woolnoth, and also on the Wednesday morning. After he was turned of seventy, he often undertook to assist other clergymen; sometimes even to the preaching six sermons in the space of a week. What was more extraordinary, he continued his usual course of preaching at his own church after he was fourscore years old, and that when he could no longer see to read his text! His memory and voice sometimes failed him; but it was remarked, that, at this great age, he was no where more collected or lively than in the pulpit. He was punctual as to time with his congregation; and preached every first Sunday evening in the month on relative duties. Mr. Alderman Lea regularly sent his carriage to convey him to the church, and Mr. Bates sent his servant to attend him in the pulpit; which friendly assistance was continued till Mr. N. could appear no longer in public.

His ministerial visits were exemplary. I do not recollect one, though favoured with many, in which his general information and lively genius did not communicate instruction, and his affectionate and condescending sympathy did not leave comfort.

Truth demands it should be said, that he did not always administer consolation, nor give an account of characters, with sufficient discrimination. His talent did not lie in "discerning of spirits." I never saw him so much moved as when any friend endeavoured to correct his errors in this respect. His credulity seemed to arise from the consciousness he had of his own integrity, and from that sort of parental fondness which he bore to all his friends, real or pretended. I knew one, since dead, whom he thus described, while living—"He is certainly an odd man, and has his failings; but he has great integrity, and I hope is going to heaven." Whereas almost all who knew him thought the man should go first into the pillory!

In his FAMILY, Mr. N. might be admired more safely than imitated. His excessive attachment to Mrs. N. is so fully displayed in his Narrative, and confirmed in the two volumes he thought proper to publish, entitled "Letters to a Wife," that the reader will need no information on this subject. Some of his friends wished this violent attachment had been cast more into the shade, as tending to furnish a spur, where human nature generally needs a curb. He used, indeed, to speak of such attachments, in the abstract, as idolatry; though his own was providentially ordered to be the main hinge on which his preservation and deliverance turned, while in his worst state. Good men, however, cannot be too cautious how they give sanction, by their expressions or example, to a passion, which, when not under sober regulation, has overwhelmed not only families, but states, with disgrace and ruin.

With his unusual degree of benevolence and affection, it was not extraordinary that the spiritual interests of his servants were brought forward, and examined severally every Sunday afternoon; and that, being treated like children, they should grow old in his service. In short, Mr. N. could live no longer than he could love; it is no wonder, therefore, if his nieces had more of his heart than is generally afforded to their own children by the fondest parents. It has already been mentioned, that his house was an asylum for the perplexed or afflicted. Young ministers were peculiarly the objects of his attention: he instructed them, he encouraged them, he warned them, and might truly be said to be a father in Christ, "spending and being spent" for the interest of his church. In order thus to execute the various avocations of the day, he used to rise early; he seldom was found abroad in the evening, and was exact in his appointments.

Of his WRITINGS, I think little need be said here; they are in wide circulation, and best speak for themselves. What I shall observe upon them, therefore, will be general and cursory.

The sermons Mr. N. published at Liverpool, after being refused on his first application for orders, were intended to show what he would have preached, had he been admitted; they are highly creditable to his understanding and to his heart. The facility with which he attained so much of the learned languages, seems partly accounted for, from his being able to acquire, so early, a neat and natural style in his own language, and that under such evident disadvantages. His Review of Ecclesiastical History, so far as it is proceeded, has been much esteemed; and, if it had done no more than excite the Rev. J. Milner (as that most valuable and instructive author informs us it did,) to pursue Mr. N.'s idea more largely, it was sufficient success. Before this, the world seems to have lost sight of a history of real christianity, and to have been content with what, for the most part, was but an account of the ambition and politics of secular men, assuming the christian name.

It must be evident to any one, who observes the spirit of all his sermons, hymns, tracts, &c. that nothing is aimed at which should be met by critical investigation. In the preface to his Hymns, he remarks, " Though I would not offend readers of taste by a wilful coarseness and negligence, I do not write professedly for them. I have simply declared my own views and feelings, as I might have done if I had composed hymns in some of the newly discovered islands in the South Sea, where no person had any knowledge of the name of Jesus but myself."

To dwell, therefore, with a critical eye on this part of his public character, would be absurd and impertinent, and to erect a tribunal to which he seems not amenable. He appears to have paid no regard to a nice ear, or an accurate reviewer; but, preferring a style at once neat and perspicuous, to have laid out himself entirely for the service of the church of God, and more especially for the tried and experienced part of its members.

His chief excellence seemed to lie in the easy and natural style of his epistolary correspondence. His letters will be read while real religion exists; and they are the best draught of his own mind.

He had so largely communicated to his friends in this way, that I have heard him say, he "thought, if his letters were collected, they would make several folios." He selected many of these for publication, and expressed a hope, that no other person would take that liberty with the rest, which were so widely spread abroad. In this, however, he was disappointed and grieved, as he once remarked to me; and for which reason I do not annex any letters that I received from him. He esteemed that collection published under the title of "Cardiphonia," as the most useful of his writings, and mentioned various instances of the benefits which he heard they had conveyed to many.

His Apologia, or defence of conformity, was written on occasion of some reflections (perhaps only jocular,) cast on him at that time His Letters to a Wife, written during his three voyages to Africa, and published in 1793, have been received with less satisfaction than most of his other writings. While, however, his advanced age and inordinate fondness may be pleaded for this publication, care should be taken lest men fall into a contrary extreme, and suppose that temper to be their wisdom, which leads them to avoid another, which they consider as his weakness. But his Messiah, before mentioned, his Letters of the Rev. Mr. Vanlier, chaplain at the

Cape, his Memoirs of the Rev. John Cowper, (brother to the poet,) and those of the Rev. Mr. Grimshaw, of Yorkshire, together with his single sermons and tracts, have been well received, and will remain a public benefit.

I recollect reading a MS. which Mr. N. lent me, containing a correspondence that had passed between himself and the Rev. Dr. Dixon, principal of St. Edmund Hall, Oxford, and another MS. of a correspondence between him and the late Rev. Martin Madan. They would have been very interesting to the public, particularly the latter, and were striking evidences of Mr. N.'s humility, piety, and faithfulness; but reasons of delicacy led him to commit the whole to the flames.

To speak of his writings in the mass, they certainly possess what many have aimed at, but very few attained, namely, originality. They are the language of the heart; they show a deep experience of its religious feelings, a continual anxiety to sympathize with man in his wants, and to direct him to his only resources.

His CONVERSATION, and familiar habits with his friends, were more peculiar amusing and instructive, than any I ever witnessed. It is difficult to convey a clear idea of them by description. His letters, and the remarks which he made in familiar conversation with his friends, so far as they have been preserved, are in harmony with the general tenor of his character, and abound in those sentiments of glowing piety which he so eminently possessed.

THE END.

AVAILABLE WHERE BOOKS ARE SOLD

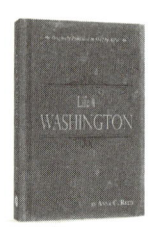

Life of Washington
5 x 7 • 290 pages
Case Bound
Retail: $16.99
978-0-89051-578-5

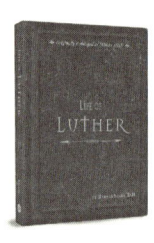

Life of Luther
5 x 7 • 496 pages
Case Bound
Retail: $17.99
978-0-89051-599-0

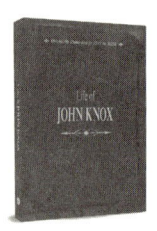

Life of John Knox
5 x 7 • 144 pages
Case Bound
Retail: $14.99
978-0-89051-602-7

Life of Andrew Jackson
5 x 7 • 400 pages
Case Bound
Retail: $19.99
978-0-89051-603-4